Dedication

To the pastors, leaders, and people at Eliot Baptist Church.
Studying the Word with you has taught me so much about being held by God.

Gratitude

I am so grateful for God's gracious provision of dedicated, kind, and wise people to help me write this book. A big thank you to my three writing prayer sisters, Amanda, Jenn, and Marlene, for encouraging me and praying so faithfully for me. Another huge thank you to Judy Wilson and Marcia Aupperlee, who spent hours reading and re-reading the manuscript, checking not only for grammatical errors, but making sure the content honored God and His Word theologically. And huge thanks to Terry Harris, Ben Santiago, and Megan Freiwald of Harris House Publishing. You three. So good at what you do and so much in love with God yourselves. I couldn't ask for a better team to help me publish this Bible Study. Most of all, thank You, Lord, for holding me as I studied Your Word with You.

Table of Contents

Hear me as I pray, O Lord.

Be merciful and answer me!

My heart has heard you say, "Come and talk with me."

And my heart responds, "Lord, I am coming."

Do not turn your back on me.

Do not reject your servant in anger.

You have always been my helper.

Don't leave me now; don't abandon me,

O God of my salvation!

Even if my father and mother abandon me,

the Lord will hold me close.

—Psalm 27:7-10

*H*eld was not the original title I planned to use for this Bible study. Before my indepth dive into the Book of Psalms last year, I had tentatively named the study *Adore*. However, as I entered into the raw, honest, melancholy, triumphant, emotional world of the Psalms, I discovered that not every psalm is a pure song of praise. Instead, each one is an honest heart cry to the God who listens and who holds us in His strong arms in the bad times as well as the good.

No matter how we feel, we can tell Him. Whether we are shouting for joy or screaming in pain, He will hear us and He will hold us if we simply fall into His waiting arms. Suffering is abundant in our world today, and it was abundant during the 900 years in which the Book of Psalms were written.[*1] Always, though, we see and feel the hold God has on us, no matter what, as we read through this amazing songbook of the Jewish nation.

Are you ready? We will discover more about who God is and how He operates in our fallen world through poetry, theology, history, lament, triumph, worship, and despair. We will enter turbulent waters, at times, as honest psalmists cry out in bewilderment to a God who seems silent. We will be shown how to praise God and be grateful even in the midst of troubles. We will learn gratitude and confession in deeper ways as we see how the men of old bared their souls to the One who made them. In short, we will see how we, as humans, can interact intimately, nestled in with the One who made us. I am excited to unpack this with you!

Held is an interactive Bible study. This means that you and I are going to examine the Book of Psalms together. It's a nine-week study with seven lessons each week. Most lessons will take no longer than twenty minutes to complete, and often you will finish in even less time. This is designed to be simple enough that you can truly create an everyday habit of meeting with God! The very psalms we are going to study proclaim the wisdom and joy that come from meeting with Him often.

1* The genre of Psalms is Songs and Poetry of all kinds. It is written by multiple authors; David wrote 73, Asaph wrote 12, the sons of Korah wrote 9, Solomon wrote 3, Ethan, and Moses each wrote one (Ps. 90), and 51 of the Psalms are anonymous. They were written over the span of approximately 900 years (Beginning at the time of Moses 1440 B.C. and through the captivity in 586 B.C.). —Smith, Jay, "Psalm," Bible Hub, https://biblehub.com/summary/psalms/

Consider these verses as we begin:

> *Oh, the joys of those who do not follow the advice of the wicked, or stand around with sinners, or join in with mockers. But they delight in the law of the LORD, **meditating on it day and night**.* —Psalm 1:1-2, emphasis mine

> *Listen to my voice in the morning, LORD. **Each morning** I bring my requests to you and wait expectantly.* —Psalm 5:3, emphasis mine

> *Joyful are people of integrity, who follow the instructions of the LORD. **Joyful are those who obey his laws and search for him with all their hearts.*** —Psalm 119:1-2, emphasis mine

It is a true joy to spend time with the Lord! Unlike humans, He has all the time in the world to listen to you and hear your heart. And He's the One who knows your heart and loves you despite some of the nasty things in there. He loved you enough to come and die for you, and He asks you to draw near to Him, to yoke yourself to Him, and to abide in Him each and every day. My desire is that your daily time with God will be your greatest treasure. That you would not drag yourself to the couch or easy chair in the morning, determined to get the study done. Instead, that you would pour that cup o' tea or coffee or lemonade and race to that special meeting place with Him. That you would be eager to learn from Him and unload your sorrows to Him, knowing that you will, indeed, be held by Him whenever you come.

The study begins each day with just you and God. I'll lead you in a prayer to focus your heart on the Lord so that you may be receptive to His words. Next, you'll do your own quiet study with Him. You'll easily be able to follow the directions. We'll then "talk" about the reading. My commentary is meant to be read after you and the Lord have spent precious time together. That time alone with Him is the most important part of your quiet time. Finally, we'll meet in the commentary to unpack the meaning of the psalm, discover more about our great God, and understand how to unburden ourselves and be real with Him.

Let's learn together how to be held.

Note about doing the group study: In the back of this book, you'll find a nine-week leader's guide for weekly meetings in a group. If you are the leader of the group, this is where you will be given direction for how to lead the study. If you are a member of the group, feel free to "peek" at the questions in advance. However, nothing needs to be written in advance from that section of the book. You'll answer the questions together during group time. During the week, just stick to your daily reading and responses. Let's keep it simple!

Additional Study Options:

Option 1. What did you learn about God?

At the end of each day's lesson, you'll see this question. If you would like to contemplate this in more depth, you'll find a section at the end of the book where you can record all you learn about God from each psalm you read. You might list His attributes, for example, or perhaps something God does. Here's what a sample list might look like:

> Plants us firmly if we meditate on His Word (Psalm 1)
>
> Shepherds us (Psalm 23)
>
> Is with us in the valley of death (Psalm 23)
>
> Knit me together in my mother's womb (Psalm 139)

Option 2. Read All the Psalms Plan

I was not able to include all 150 psalms in this 9-week study. When we study something devotionally, we focus on a small portion of Scripture and meditate on it, reading it several times. In order to do all the psalms in that slow, meditative way, the study would have to be much longer. However, some will have the extra time and desire to read our "main" psalm as well as another psalm or two. If that is you, the Read All the Psalms Plan will help you. At the end of each assignment, I'll let you know what additional chapters to read that day in order to read them all. This is optional, so don't feel pressured to do this. But if you'd like to do it, the plan will show you how. *Helpful note, if you opt for this:* You may want to look at the additional reading plan at the start of each day's assignment so that you can read the psalms in order.

A psalm is a song. It's meant to be sung in worship or in solitude, or perhaps whispered in times of great distress. There are 150 psalms in the Bible book called Psalms. Within that book, the psalms are divided into smaller "books" or groups. Although several interesting theories exist, the Bible itself gives no definitive reason for the divisions. If this interests you (or your group if you are doing a group study), I encourage you to dig deeper on your own and examine some of the theories. Whether or not there are deeper reasons, at the very least, these smaller book divisions made it easier for people to find a certain psalm to sing if they knew which "book" it came from! I'll let you know which book we are in as we progress through the psalms, but we won't really be discussing them further than that for our purposes.

Today we begin Book One of the Psalms and, with it, our nine-week adventure together! One of my dearest hopes for you is that during this time you will develop a rock-solid habit of meeting with God daily. I've found that this happy time with Him enables me to face the day with more joy and wisdom than if I try to stumble through it on my own.

Choose a place in your home that is best for you to meet with God. Place your Bible, journal, and this book with two pens in a basket or tote bag and keep them right there by your place. Then, when you sit down, you will have everything you need except, perhaps, that cup o' tea or coffee that will need to be made fresh, of course. Meeting with God daily ought to be a thrill, not a duty. We have the privilege of entering into the presence of the living God and hearing from Him personally through His Word. May this time become more and more precious to you day by day.

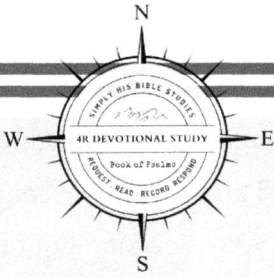

Psalm 1

Request: Father God, as I start this study of the "songbook" of the Bible, help me learn more about You. Teach me how to share my heart with You more as I study how the psalmists did so. Reveal Your specific word to me today as I read the very first psalm. Guide me, please. In Jesus' Name, Amen.

Read: Psalm 1

Record: Write down one verse from the passage that stood out to you.

Respond: Write a short prayer, talking to God about that verse.

Our very first psalm is a teaching psalm. It's a perfect way to begin our study in this incredible book of the Bible. Psalm 1 teaches us to value reading God's words to us. This is such an encouragement right out of the gate! Did you have a hard time choosing the verse that stood out to you? Sometimes, several verses stand out to me, and it takes me a few moments to choose just one. I wish we lived near each other and you could just run next door and share with me what you chose!

Let's see what we can learn from this psalm. Two types of people are contrasted here: the wicked and the godly. What do we learn in this passage about being godly? It's stunning how many lessons can be found in such a short little psalm. Here are the lessons I gleaned about the godly:

- The godly are blessed and filled with joy when they choose the good path. I love that! Joy follows obedience.

- The godly do not take advice from just anyone. They avoid advice from those who are wicked, the ones who take no interest in God and His ways.

- The godly don't hang out with sinners and join in with mockers. Their closest friends are not those who disdain the Lord and His ways.

- The godly are delighted with God's Word. They value it and meditate on it constantly.

- The godly plant themselves firmly in places where they can learn from God. They soak up the living water of the Word and are satisfied.

- The godly don't shrivel or wither. They're held steady by the words of truth and their faith in those words. Therefore, they prosper.

- The godly are blessed to have the Lord watching over them, guiding them to the right decisions and the path that will lead to blessing.

The wicked can also teach us a lesson or three. Here's the fate of those who ignore, disdain, or even mock the God who made them:

- The wicked band together and encourage each other's folly.

- The wicked are like chaff. They have no weight or substance to them. They are easily swayed from one thought to another, and they have no firm foundation.

- The wicked walk toward sure destruction.

So. That was clear. It really is better to be godly. Our first psalm wants us to pursue godliness by immersing ourselves in the Word of God. The Bible is like no other book. It is the Living Word of the one true God. When we read it, seeking to hear God's voice through its pages, we are changed.

Oh, I am so glad you chose to do this study with me! I believe you and I will be changed as we seek the Lord each day in our readings, asking Him to highlight the personal life lessons we need for our particular season of life. May God move in your heart, stir your soul, and draw you ever nearer to Him as you study this book. *Be held.*

My verse: "Oh, the joys of those who do not follow the advice of the wicked, or stand around with sinners, or join in with mockers" (Psalm 1:1).

My response: Father God, I'm thankful that turning away from bad and evil choices results in blessing and joy—not just one joy, but multiple joys! Father, obedience to You is joyful. We can experience life without secrets, deceptions, and shame. We have freedom in You. Thank You, Lord, for the joys.

Additional Study Options:

What did you learn about God from Psalm 1? Start your list in the Study Notes section at the back of this book or in your own journal.

Read All the Psalms Plan: Read Psalms 2-3.

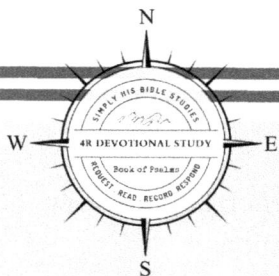

Psalm 5

Request: Dear Lord, I thank You for this new day to learn and grow closer to You. Help me, like the godly in Psalm 1, to hunger for Your teaching this morning. Enable me to remember throughout the day all I have read, meditating on it and planting myself in Your truths. In Jesus' Name, Amen.

Read: Psalm 5

Record: Write down one verse from the passage that stood out to you.

Respond: Write a short prayer, talking to God about that verse.

Our psalm today was written by King David, the most prolific of our psalm writers. He is named the writer of 73 of the 150 psalms in the Book of Psalms, but many scholars attribute other psalms to him as well. One source I read attributed 88 to David! He started life as the youngest son of Jesse, and his job was to watch the sheep. He spent many days alone in the wilderness, and he clearly used his time productively. He played the harp and wrote songs to the Lord long before he became a famous (and infamous) king. I think all that time alone with God, with a heart that wanted to know God, is what gave David his beautiful poetic words in these wonderful songs. Our psalm for today even has directions attached suggesting what musical instrument ought to be played with it. David favored the flute for this worshipful praise song.

As we read, we discover that this psalm is composed of many various elements. David starts with a cry and a groan for help. "O LORD, hear me as I pray; pay attention to my groaning" (Psalm 5:1). David wasn't shy about his complaints and his needs. He ran directly to God in times of trouble, and he models that for us here. It's okay to cry out to God and to groan. The psalms teach us this over and over again. David prays for answers and lays his requests before God. We can, too.

Second, David communicates anxiety about enemies. He often mentions wicked enemies in the psalms he writes. He had plenty of them, starting from his earliest days. As a shepherd boy, he fought off wild animals bent on harming the sheep. Later, he fought Goliath, the champion of the Philistines and a deadly enemy by his looks. No one expected teenage David to win that round, but he did with God's help and strength. He was chased down countless times by Saul, the king before him. Many were the men who would gladly have told King Saul where David was hiding in order to get a reward. David had to be very careful whom he trusted. And, as king, David had many enemies, as well. Some were even members of his own family. David didn't pretend with God. He named his enemies and asked for help with them. We can do that, too.

Third, we read praise and adoration in this psalm and so many others. David reminds himself, through his song-prayer, of just how great our God is and just how worthy He is to be praised. We learn so much about God through Psalm 5. God's love is unfailing. So different from human love that waxes and wanes. God's presence in the temple produces awe and reverence in us. When we go to God, He spreads His protection over us, and we find sweet refuge. God fills us with joy. We can nestle in and be held. Oh, what a God we serve!

All this in a few short verses! I love how the topics and mood can change and shift so rapidly in these psalms. It reassures me that my prayers can be spontaneous and real—from my heart, spilling out in whatever order I am feeling them. God wants me to be the real "me" when I speak to Him. I don't have to sound fancy or even stay on topic. All thoughts are welcomed as I run into His shelter. Oh, how I praise and thank Him for that privilege granted to me, His child.

My verse: "Listen to my cry for help, my King and my God, for I pray to no one but you" (Psalm 5:2).

My response: There is no god but You. You are God! You are King. Help me, Lord, to knock down any idol I've elevated. Help me look only to You today and every day for help, for refuge, and for strength.

Additional Study Options:

What did you learn about God from Psalm 5? Add to your list in the Study Notes section at the back of this book or in your own journal.

Read All the Psalms Plan: Read Psalms 4, 6.

Psalm 8

Request: Teach me, Lord. Show me how to worship You and honor You as I read this psalm today. In Jesus' Name, Amen.

Read: Psalm 8

Record: Write down one verse from this passage that stood out to you.

Respond: Write a short prayer, talking to God about that verse.

_____

_____

_____

_____

_____

_____

_____

_____

Today, we were treated to a psalm that was pure praise. Wasn't it a glorious read? Based on what David wrote, I have to believe that he wrote it after a night of stargazing. Oh, how I wish I could see the night sky the way David saw it. In my opinion, one of the saddest consequences of electric lights has been the loss of the fullness of a star-studded sky. Don't get me wrong. I truly appreciate electricity. However, it does rob us of some of the magnificence humans in other centuries witnessed when their view did not have to compete with artificial light.

Have you ever been in a place where you could see more stars than you could possibly count? I have. I was in Arkansas, speaking at a retreat being held in a stately home that had been used as a hunting lodge. This lodge was surrounded by corn fields. Miles and miles of them. So, once the evening talk was done, I decided to walk waaaaay out in those fields where the lights from the lodge did not compete with the stars of the night sky. I looked up.

Wow. Just wow.

The splendor of the sky took my breath away. It was magnificent. I soaked it in, but then the mosquitoes found me. There seemed to be as many of them as there were stars, and I raced back toward the lodge! However, it was worth every mosquito bite to witness that sky.

I love that God made the sky so vast and so filled with mysterious stars, planets, comets, galaxies, and even black holes—whatever they are. He communicates His immensity through a sky that everyone on the planet can see. Rich or poor, happy or sad, we all have the privilege of looking up. Even in our light-polluted world, the moon still shines down on us, and the sun still paints the sky pinks and purples at dawn and dusk. It's amazing to see, and every sky is different. Our God is so creative!

David is bursting with praise and wonder as he reflects on the night sky in this psalm. It also humbles him. Who are we in comparison to those lights up there and the vastness of it all? Have you ever felt that way? How is it possible that the God who made All This, plus billions of people, actually cares about me? And yet, He does. "And the very hairs on your head are all numbered" (Luke 12:7a).

Today, let's sit in awe of the wonder of His love for little us. And, if you have time, go back and read Psalm 8 out loud to the One who made you and cares so deeply for you!

My verse: "O LORD, our Lord, your majestic name fills the earth" (Psalm 8:9a).

My response: You are the one true God. LORD of all. The great I Am. You are the One to whom I gladly give my allegiance. You are King. And all creation shouts Your Name. Hallelujah!

Additional Study Options:

What did you learn about God from Psalm 8? Add to your list in the Study Notes section at the back of this book or in your own journal.

Read All the Psalms Plan: Read Psalm 7.

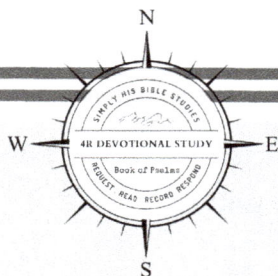

Psalm 10

Request: Father, draw me near today as I open Your Living Word. Help me to listen, learn, and grow as I study. In Jesus' Name, Amen.

Read: Psalm 10

Record: Write down one verse from this passage that stood out to you.

Respond: Write a short prayer, talking to God about that verse.

_____

_____

_____

_____

_____

_____

_____

_____

_____

Why? That's the question asked in this psalm, and it's a question people have asked through the centuries. We've moved from praise and adoration in Psalm 8 to a confused and hurting voice in Psalm 10. Our unnamed psalmist has expected things to go a certain way, and they have not. He expected God to always feel close. He expected that the wicked would be punished quickly. He expected that the helpless would be swiftly helped. In short, he wants a tidy world, where good people are happy, and bad people are punished, and God always comes through exactly the way he thinks He should.

Ever had expectations like that dashed? I surely have. I've prayed for little babies to live and instead endured the sorrow of those close to me losing eight tiny ones. I've prayed for marriages to be restored and watched them end in divorce. I've prayed for happy endings and seen grief instead. I bet you have had times like that, too. God does not always respond the way we wish He would. That's the hard, honest truth. It's one reason I am so drawn to the psalms. They're real. When the psalmist is happy, he shouts it to the skies. When he's bewildered and feeling betrayed, he grieves and laments.

And God Himself allows both the praise and the lament. We learn through reading all the emotional highs and lows of the psalms that God welcomes us to come near no matter what we are feeling. Even if we are feeling disappointed in Him! I've come to Him in my disappointment and figuratively beat on His chest and screamed, "Why?" He's never turned me away. Instead, He's held me close and grieved with me for a world that will not turn to Him and willfully goes its own sinful way.

And therein lies part of the answer to the question of why. I will not presume to fully answer the question of why bad things happen to seemingly good people, while fortune and success can often come to really bad people. However, I do know this. God values our love highly. He wants us to genuinely love Him. This means we have to be free to *not* love Him and to do evil instead of good. He's willing to allow evil to temporarily flourish in order to give all people—even the ones we would call very evil—a chance to repent and turn to Him and be changed. Without that freedom to choose to love Him, we would all be robotic and non-human. Our God desires our heartfelt, freely chosen love. He's pursued us at great cost.

Despite the author's pain and frustration, he knows that at the heart of the matter, God exists and He is good. He declares in verse 14, after lamenting all the wickedness that is running rampant, "But you see the trouble and grief they (the wicked) cause. You take note of it and punish them. The helpless put their trust in you. You defend the orphans." This faith—to know that God sees and will punish the wicked in His time—is beautiful. God is so pleased with us when we continue to trust Him even when nothing is going right. He's told us it ends well. It will. Let's believe Him even when we don't currently see that happy ending on the horizon.

Let's not be afraid to lament, to cry, to tell Him our sorrows honestly. He sees our hearts. He's not shocked by our words. He wants us to draw near to Him, grieving yet trusting that His plans are ultimately for good, believing that someday all will be made right when Jesus returns. Let's run *toward* Him with the why. He alone has the answers, and He alone can bring the comfort we need.

My verse: "But you see the trouble and grief they cause. You take note of it and punish them. The helpless put their trust in you. You defend the orphans" (Psalm 10:14).

My response: Lord, help me to remember when I see evil flourish that You also see it, and You will avenge. Thank You that You are never on evil's side but always near to the helpless and the orphans. Oh, Lord—Your permanent goodness is my joy and my sure hope when the world looks bleak.

Additional Study Options:

What did you learn about God from Psalm 10? Add to your list in the Study Notes section at the back of this book or in your own journal.

Read All the Psalms Plan: Read Psalm 9.

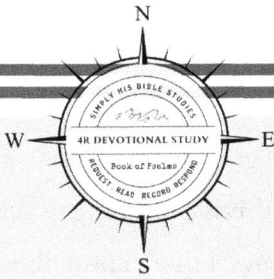

Psalm 11

Request: Heavenly Father, open my heart to what You would teach me through Your Word this morning. Enable me to take Your teaching with me as I go about my days, putting into practice what You show me. Thank You, Lord, for Your living presence right here, right now. In Jesus' Name, Amen.

Read: Psalm 11

Record: Write down one verse from this passage that stood out to you.

Respond: Write a short prayer, talking to God about that verse.

David starts this psalm with an excellent subject sentence: "I trust in the LORD for protection" (Psalm 11:1a). Not every psalm is as tidy as this one. This one would get a good grade in my high school English teacher's class. In a sense, although David personalizes it, this is a teaching psalm. David shows us why and how we can trust God for protection in scary times. I don't know about you, but I feel like we are living in scary times right now. I guess every generation feels this way as every generation faces the threat of war, disease, famine, and natural disasters. We humans are pretty fragile. We can get knocked down and knocked out pretty easily in a lot of different ways. So, this psalm today is for us.

In verses 1-3, David begins by laying out the dilemma. The wicked are abundant, and they are aiming at us. "They shoot from the shadows" and aim at the good guys, as my translation describes it. If someone is shooting from the shadows, they are hidden. It makes us a bit jumpy, wondering where the arrows are coming from. We can get blindsided by evil in many ways. I still feel a sense of shock when I read about a doctor who mistreated a patient or a politician who outright lied. This should not be! I should be able to trust doctors and politicians whom I've elected. My sense of stability wobbles when an evildoer is exposed.

After David lays out the dilemma and dismisses the argument that one should flee for safety in a panic, he speaks truth to us. The last four verses in this psalm are meant to calm. We do not need to freak out because life here is hard and uncertain. Why? Well, because what is certain matters far more!

God still rules in Heaven. He is in His holy temple, and He is not wringing His hands, worried about what's happening on earth. He sees from the beginning to the end, and He knows it ends well. All things will one day be made right. If He's not wringing His hands in despair but calmly watching His great plan unfold, we do not need to hand-wring either!

God sees everyone and every wicked deed. Even though it looks like the bad guys are winning, they are not. They will die. They are subject to the same threats of war, disease, famine, and natural disasters that we are. And once they die, they will face the God who sits on the throne and sees. It will not go well for them. Verse six is a pretty angry verse: "He will rain down blazing coals and burning sulfur on the wicked, punishing them with scorching winds" (Psalm 11:6). Ultimately, it's a terrible idea to be wicked. Don't do it. You're always looking over your shoulder, fearing assault from someone you harmed. When you die, it gets worse. Much worse. We really don't need to fear the wicked. Instead, we ought to be praying for them to turn and change!

I love David's concluding words to us. We who love God and turn to Him will someday see His face! This same big God who is seated on His throne, able to punish the wicked, wants to draw us close. We will be welcomed into heaven someday, not on our own merits, but simply because we chose to accept Jesus' death on our behalf. With that choice, we receive forgiveness of sins, turn our hearts over to Him, and call Him Lord. There is no need to worry. God's got this. Whenever the panic starts, just picture Him seated on His throne and remember that it ends well for anyone and everyone who puts their trust in Him. Aaaaahhh. I feel better already!

My verse: "The LORD examines both the righteous and the wicked. He hates those who love violence" (Psalm 11:5).

My response: Oh, Father God, You are filled with love and patience and compassion. No wonder You get angry at those who are cruel and violent!

Additional Study Options:

What did you learn about God from Psalm 11? Add to your list in the Study Notes section at the back of this book or in your own journal.

Read All the Psalms Plan: Read Psalms 12-13.

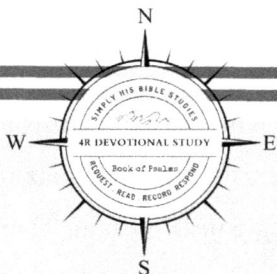

Psalm 16

Request: Holy God, seated on the Throne, I come to You today so thankful that You hold everything in Your competent hands. Nothing can ever harm me in the long run. The worst that can happen leads to the best—eternal life with You! Please teach me today. In Jesus' Name, Amen.

Read: Psalm 16

Record: Write down one verse from this passage that stood out to you.

Respond: Write a short prayer, talking to God about that verse.

What a beautiful psalm! Did it quiet your soul and make you want to nestle close? I felt safer just reading it. I love that this psalm is a reminder of how good and near our God is! We can sometimes feel He is very far away. Particularly if we've asked (begged!) for something without sensing any response from Him, or when we are experiencing trouble after trouble. There are seasons like that, aren't there? The year you needed surgery, your mom died, and your husband lost his job. That kind of season. In good times and bad times, we need psalms to remind us of who God is despite what we might be seeing or feeling in our temporary troubles.

One of the optional study choices each day is to keep a list of what you are learning about God. Today, let's keep a list together based on what David teaches us in Psalm 16.

- God welcomes us to come to Him for refuge.
- God is our Master. He is in charge, and we are not.
- Every good thing we have comes from the One who created everything. Our God. (See James 1:17)
- God Himself is our inheritance. Any possession we have here on earth will ultimately disintegrate. But we have an inheritance that is permanent. We will always be loved if we have asked Jesus to forgive us, save us and enter us through His Spirit.
- God blesses us.
- God guards what is ours eternally.
- God is always with us, night and day.
- God is steady, firm. When we are clinging to Him, we cannot be shaken.
- God enables us to rest because of His protection.
- God will raise us from the dead. Death is really an indication that new life in Heaven is about to begin. Adventure beyond our wildest imaginings is about to commence! Death has lost its sting.
- God shows us the way of life.
- God's presence brings us *joy*.
- Living with God forever will be our greatest pleasure.

My verse: "LORD, you alone are my inheritance, my cup of blessing. You guard all that is mine" (Psalm 16:5).

My response: Father God, how I thank You for loving me, holding me, guarding me. You are always with me, and I'll never be without Your love. My cup overflows!

Additional Study Options:

What did you learn about God from Psalm 16? Add to your list in the Study Notes section at the back of this book or in your own journal.

Read All the Psalms Plan: Read Psalms 14-15.

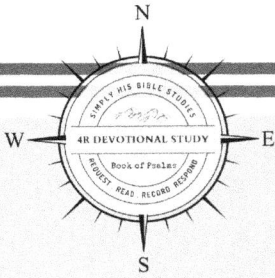

N
W E
S

SIMPLY HIS BIBLE STUDIES
4R DEVOTIONAL STUDY
Book of Psalms
REQUEST READ RECORD RESPOND

Psalm 18

Request: Oh, Father God! What an honor it is to sit before You like this, opening Your Living Word, and asking for Your specific guidance for little me. How is it possible that You, who run the galaxies, will stop to hear my prayers and teach me the way I should go? And yet, You do. Make me aware today of this privilege, and please illuminate Your Word as I read it. In Jesus' Name, Amen.

Read: Psalm 18

Record: Write down one verse from this passage that stood out to you.

Respond: Write a short prayer, talking to God about that verse.

The psalm we read today is anchored in history. It's kinda fun to know why and when King David wrote this triumphant psalm of praise and thanksgiving! My Bible phrases the history part like this: "A psalm of David, the servant of the LORD. He sang this song to the LORD on the day the LORD rescued him from all his enemies and from Saul." Couldn't you just feel the joy and WOW factor as David praised God in Psalm 18?

Let's review why David would write such a triumphant song. Perhaps it's because the road to becoming king was anything but easy. David was anointed by Samuel when he was just a boy. He was basically told through that anointing that someday he would be the king of Israel. However, after that anointing, he simply went back to watching sheep. There was no immediate glory. David showed unbelievable faith in God as a teenager when he fought his epic battle with Goliath and won. Scholars believe he was between the ages of 15 and 20, not yet conscripted to serve in the army. Instead of that victory catapulting him to kingship, however, David instead served under Saul in the army. According to 2 Samuel 5:4, David did not become king until he was thirty. There were a lot of years of waiting, and they were rocky years. No wonder he wrote a song, our psalm today, to commemorate the day when Samuel's anointing became reality. In between, there were many hardships that made the final fulfillment an unlikely triumph. Let's continue our review and see why this psalm was so important.

After David served in many battles that resulted in great victories, King Saul became jealous of David's fame and popularity. Oh, be careful of jealousy and comparison! Once it takes root, we become bitter, nasty people, and we do things we could never have imagined we'd do! Saul mercilessly hunted David, desiring to kill him. Twice, he threw a spear at David within his own palace, trying to kill him. Saul even took away David's wife and made her marry another man. Saul was mad with hatred and a twisted desire to eliminate his competition.

David, on the other hand, spared Saul's life when it was within his power to kill him, and he scolded anyone who spoke badly of King Saul. He believed Saul was God's anointed until the time God chose to make David king instead. David was faithful to God and even wrote songs of praise to Him, while living in caves, scrounging for food, and running for his life continually. David believed God even when all the evidence shouted that he had been deserted by God and that His promise to make him king was not going to come true. Now, that's faith.

I want faith like that. Faith that believes, even when I am waiting and waiting and not seeing God's hand at work. Faith that God is still good, still working, still loving and holding me. Faith that remains even when I am stuck in a hard place and quite frankly do not like His plan for my life or how it is unfolding. You know what helps me have that kind of faith? Psalm 18. It highlights the joy, the relief, the gratitude of a man who held on to God's promises in the worst of circumstances. David came through a long, dark night and into morning glory! I love Psalm 18. Let's be like David and have faith in the hard times, knowing the morning will, indeed, come.

My verse: "But in my distress I cried out to the LORD; yes, I prayed to my God for help. He heard me from his sanctuary; my cry to him reached his ears" (Psalm 18:6).

My response: Oh, Father, even in times of great distress when all seems hopeless, help me to still cry out! You are the One who rescues even in the impossible situations. Help me to always look to You—no matter what.

Additional Study Options:

What did you learn about God from Psalm 18? Add to your list in the Study Notes section at the back of this book or in your own journal.

Read All the Psalms Plan: Read Psalm 17.

How has your daily time with God progressed this past week? I hope you have found a rhythm to your days that includes this sweet time with the Lord and His Word. If you are still trying to find that rhythm, don't give up! It takes a long time to form a habit. Each time you do manage to sit down and meet with God, it helps the habit grow. And when you do miss a day? *Grace.* God gives grace in abundance. Just try again. This week holds so much goodness as we look at new psalms. I hope you enjoy and learn and grow each day.

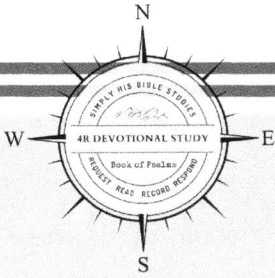

N
W — E
S

SIMPLY HIS BIBLE STUDIES
4R DEVOTIONAL STUDY
Book of Psalms
REQUEST READ RECORD RESPOND

Psalm 19

Request: Father, as I start a new week of studying Your songbook, the Psalms, would you please give me joy and focus as I study? I love meeting with You. Help me to know You better because of this time with You and to love You more and more. In Jesus' Name, Amen.

Read: Psalm 19

Record: Write down one verse from this passage that stood out to you.

Respond: Write a short prayer, talking to God about that verse.

We start our second week with one of David's beautiful psalms. Parts of Psalm 19 echo Psalm 8 as David is again in awe of the majesty of the sky. Day and night, "the heavens proclaim the glory of God. The skies display his craftsmanship" (Psalm 19:1). I have found that one of the greatest blessings in my life is something that used to feel like an annoyance. I take our little dog Bella out each night right before bed whether the weather is nice or not. And every night, I get to look up and see the moon or stars or swirling clouds. It's become a silent benediction to my day. I love looking up!

David establishes the craftsmanship of God as he describes the sky, spending quite a bit of time marveling at the precision of the sun that never fails to reappear at the appointed time. He then points us to God's perfect instructions found in the Bible. For David, it was the Old Testament books that were written at that time. Most of the prophetic books came later. Just as God is perfect in giving us night and day, season after season, God is perfect in His law and His commands. The One who made the universe can be trusted with His words in Scripture as well.

David is entranced by God's words and how helpful they are. In my translation, they are described as perfect, reviving, trustworthy, able to make wise the simple, right, joy-giving, clear, insightful, pure, true, fair, more desirable than gold, sweeter than honey, a warning to guide us, and a great reward to all who obey them. Wow. That's a pretty strong recommendation! How I want to value the Bible like this, treasuring these words and storing them up in my heart! We are blessed that the Bible is so readily available to us in this country. There are people on this planet who are so hungry for the Bible that they are willing to risk their lives for even a scrap from it. We get to read it in multiple translations whenever we want. Let's not take this great treasure for granted.

David ends this psalm in complete humility. He's just meditated on the powerful God who made our world and who gave us His Word. Now, he realizes how far he is from perfection. How much he needs cleansing and help to become more pure like God. His beautiful prayer at the end asks God to help him with the words he speaks and the thoughts he thinks. May we ask for the same so that we might please the God who loves us and has redeemed us!.

My verse(s): "The heavens proclaim the glory of God. The skies display his craftsmanship. Day after day they continue to speak; night after night they make him known" (Psalm 19:1-2).

My response: Lord, help me to continually look up! To take time to admire the vastness of the night sky. To admire clouds and seasons and rhythms in the sky. You speak through Your creation. Help me to notice it and see Your vastness and beauty displayed in what You've made!

Additional Study Options:

What did you learn about God from Psalm 19? Add to your list in the Study Notes section at the back of this book or in your own journal.

Read All the Psalms Plan: Read Psalm 20.

Psalm 22

Request: Heavenly Father, as I read Your Word and go about my day, I pray with David from Psalm 19:14. "May the words of my mouth and the meditation of my heart be pleasing to you, O LORD, my rock and my redeemer." In Jesus' Name, Amen.

Read: Psalm 22

Record: Write down one verse from this passage that stood out to you.

Respond: Write a short prayer, talking to God about that verse.

Oh, my! The significance of Psalm 22 is immense! Did you notice that opening phrase that was repeated by Jesus on the cross? We will read these words again in the gospel of Matthew, "At about three o'clock, Jesus called out with a loud voice, *'Eli, Eli, lema sabachthani?'* which means 'My God, my God, why have you abandoned me?'" (Matthew 27:46).

I am so curious about this psalm. What was David going through when he wrote it? Was God writing it with him, anticipating a time when His Son would also feel abandoned? So much of what Jesus went through is embedded in David's words. They seem prophetic with their fulfillment coming during Jesus' life. Read these examples below and marvel at what David saw and felt centuries before Jesus lived it!

Jesus was mocked and challenged to rescue Himself.

> The leading priests, the teachers of religious law, and the elders also mocked Jesus. "He saved others," they scoffed, "but he can't save himself! So he is the King of Israel, is he? Let him come down from the cross right now, and we will believe in him! He trusted God, so let God rescue him now if he wants him! For he said, 'I am the Son of God.'" Even the revolutionaries who were crucified with him ridiculed him in the same way. —Matthew 27:41-44

> Everyone who sees me mocks me. They sneer and shake their heads, saying, "Is this the one who relies on the LORD? Then let the LORD save him! If the LORD loves him so much, let the LORD rescue him!" —Psalm 22:7-8

Lots were cast for Jesus' robe at His crucifixion.

> When the soldiers had crucified Jesus, they divided his clothes among the four of them. They also took his robe, but it was seamless, woven in one piece from top to bottom. So they said, "Rather than tearing it apart, let's throw dice for it." This fulfilled the Scripture that says, "They divided my garments among themselves and threw dice for my clothing." So that is what they did. —John 19:23-24

They divide my garments among themselves and throw dice for my clothing. —Psalm 22:18

Jesus' thirst was intense.

Jesus knew that his mission was now finished, and to fulfill Scripture he said, "I am thirsty." A jar of sour wine was sitting there, so they soaked a sponge in it, put it on a hyssop branch, and held it up to his lips. —John 19:28-29

My strength has dried up like sunbaked clay. My tongue sticks to the roof of my mouth. You have laid me in the dust and left me for dead. —Psalm 22:15

Jesus was pierced by nails and that is how He hung on the cross.

Then the soldiers nailed him to the cross. —Mark 15:24a

One of the twelve disciples, Thomas (nicknamed the Twin), was not with the others when Jesus came. They told him, "We have seen the Lord!" But he replied, "I won't believe it unless I see the nail wounds in his hands, put my fingers into them, and place my hand into the wound in his side." —John 20:24-25

My enemies surround me like a pack of dogs; an evil gang closes in on me. They have pierced my hands and feet. —Psalm 22:16

Jesus had no broken bones. Water flowed from His side when He was pierced.

But when they came to Jesus, they saw that he was already dead, so they didn't break his legs. One of the soldiers, however, pierced his side with a spear, and immediately blood and water flowed out. —John 19:33-34

My life is poured out like water, and all my bones are out of joint. —Psalm 22:14a

One day every knee will bow to the Lord Jesus.

> And then I heard every creature in heaven and on earth and under the earth and in the sea. They sang: "Blessing and honor and glory and power belong to the one sitting on the throne and to the Lamb forever and ever." —Revelation 5:13

> The whole earth will acknowledge the LORD and return to him. All the families of the nations will bow down before him. For royal power belongs to the Lord. He rules all the nations. —Psalm 22:27-28

David gave voice to the agony the Lord Jesus felt on the cross in this set-apart prophetic psalm. He also pointed to a triumphant ending. I'm in awe. Can you imagine the disciples, as they began to study the Scriptures after Jesus' death and resurrection, coming to Psalm 22? They must have been filled with excitement and wonder. There it was, written hundreds of years earlier—the death of the Lamb of God, who took our sins on Himself and endured the punishment we deserved. And someday, the reigning King would return!.

My verse: "The poor will eat and be satisfied. All who seek the LORD will praise him. Their hearts will rejoice with everlasting joy" (Psalm 22:26).

My response: Lord, I love this determined burst of faith in what will take place—even though David is currently feeling abandoned and near death. To proclaim that You will be acknowledged as LORD and all will be made right, even when the present is a nightmare? That's rock-solid faith. Help me to do as David did, knowing You ultimately will rescue and restore us!

Additional Study Options:

What do you learn about God from Psalm 22? Add to your list in the Study Notes section at the back of this book or in your own journal.

Read All the Psalms Plan: Read Psalm 21.

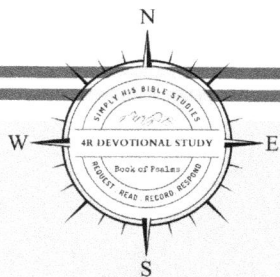

Psalm 23

Request: Heavenly Father, as I read this familiar psalm, help me to savor it, delighting in all the ways You shepherd me. I am Yours, Lord, and will someday dwell in Your house forever. In Jesus' Name, Amen.

Read: Psalm 23

Record: Write down one verse from this passage that stood out to you.

Respond: Write a short prayer, talking to God about that verse.

A long time ago, I had a memorable encounter with a shepherd in Stuttgart, Germany. My husband was in the military, and we were stationed there from 1990-1992. We lived in tall, cement-block apartment buildings that weren't very attractive. However, these buildings formed a half circle around a huge and beautiful field. This field made up for the ugly buildings with its gently rolling slopes and small copses of trees scattered about. On the opposite side of the circle, there was a highway with a stoplight. Twice a day, the light turned red to enable a shepherd to lead his sheep across that busy road to graze in the field and then return at night.

I was homeschooling our two little girls at that time, and we loved those sheep! We spent many a lunch break out in that field wandering freely. This kind shepherd allowed the girls to hold the baby lambs in the spring with his help. He did not mind them walking in the middle of the herd at will. What a joy those days were!

This kind shepherd turned fierce one very memorable day. By mistake, I left our apartment door open a second too long, and Tank, our chow/shepherd dog dashed outside and into the field amidst the placid sheep. Instinct took over. Tank started herding the sheep, racing back and forth behind them, pushing them toward that busy highway. I shouted and screamed to no avail. Tank was in his newly discovered herding happy place and paid no attention to me whatsoever.

Thankfully, the shepherd was on the watch. Within half a minute, he had risen to his feet and was shouting commands at his own sheepdog. He raced to the other side of that poor, frightened herd and kept them from the highway. I finally caught up with my renegade dog, grabbed him by the collar, and apologized in my poor German. The shepherd answered fiercely, and it was clear he was shaken and angry. I can only imagine what he was saying, and I think I am glad I could not understand him. I slunk away, towing my dog behind me, mortified and grateful that it hadn't been worse.

Here are a few lessons from my story and from David's beautiful psalm. First, sheep need a shepherd. Without guidance, they (and we) quickly go astray, led by fear toward danger and foolishness. Second, a good shepherd is always watching out for the sheep. Third, a good shepherd is both gentle with his flock and fierce with the flock's enemies. This is why we are so blessed to have a good Shepherd!

Let's stay close to Him, shall we? There are a lot of dangers out there, and when we stay close, even walking through the valley of the shadow of death is no cause for panic. He goes with us.

My verse: "He renews my strength. He guides me along right paths, bringing honor to his name" (Psalm 23:3).

My response: Lord, You are teaching me so much about strength. It comes from You. I can't manufacture it on my own, and when I am weary, I look to You for renewal. You are my strength, Mighty God! Help me to remember this in my weaknesses.

Additional Study Options:

What do you learn about God from Psalm 23? Add to your list in the Study Notes section at the back of this book or in your own journal.

Read All the Psalms Plan: Read Psalm 24.

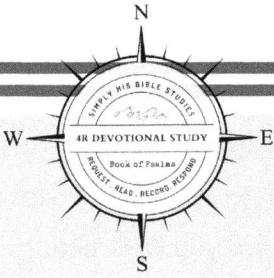

Psalm 25

Request: Oh, my Shepherd, my God, my King! Thank You for these precious moments with You where I can sit and learn and listen. Thank You for leading me by still waters and restoring my soul. I am so glad to be a part of Your flock! In Jesus' Name, Amen.

Read: Psalm 25

Record: Write down one verse from this passage that stood out to you.

Respond: Write a short prayer, talking to God about that verse.

There are times in life when decision-making is difficult and scary. Ever been in a place where you felt like a decision could have disastrous consequences if you didn't get it right? Perhaps it was a decision about whether or not to have a medical procedure. Perhaps you were choosing between two jobs, or two locations, or even two people who wanted to date you. When you looked ahead into the future, you could see potential disasters in both directions. Which path was the right path? You just didn't know, and that was a scary place to be.

My husband Ray has said at different times in our married life, "If only God would put it on a neon sign in the sky so I know what He wants me to do!" Today in Psalm 25, our David is facing a decision. "Show me the right path, O LORD; point out the road for me to follow" (Psalm 25:4). Let's learn from David. Let's see what he did and what we can do when facing a difficult decision.

First and foremost, David reaffirms his loyalty to God. His life is God's. His trust is in God. We should always begin by reminding ourselves, even speaking out loud to God, that we are His. He is ultimately responsible for our lives because we have placed them in His care. That takes some of the weight off of us right there!

Next, David lays out his problem. He has enemies trying to defeat him, and they are fierce. He does not want to be humiliated by them or deceived by them. We need to come to God in prayer with the problem and lay it out before Him. Yes, He already knows. However, He tells us over and over to come to Him and ask. So. We ask. We don't fret about the problem. We bring it to the only One who knows the right answer.

Then, David asks for advice to know the right path. He wants to know the truth about his situation so as to not be deceived into a wrong move. He reiterates that his hope is in God and that God alone is his salvation. He reminds himself that God is compassionate and full of unfailing love. He expresses gratitude that God has forgiven his sins and sees David in light of His great mercy.

This is actually an important point. Satan can often derail us when we are praying by bringing up sins committed long ago and making us feel unworthy or unable to hear from God because of them. This is a lie and a deception from the one who is called a deceiver and accuser in the Bible. If we have confessed that sin, God forgave it, and *it's done*. We can ask for help. "There is no condemnation for those who are in Christ Jesus," says Paul in Romans 8:1. Let's believe that truth and not the lies.

David continues to pray, asking for God's help and reminding himself of God's greatness and graciousness. We don't get to see God's answer or what path David took. Do you know what I think? I think that God led David along the right path because David's heart was yielded to Him. Sometimes, when I don't get a clear answer after I've prayed and yielded my will to the Spirit, I just step out. I trust God to shut the door and turn me around if I choose the wrong path. If not? I keep walking in the sure knowledge that because I asked, God is with me on the path.

My verse: "He leads the humble in doing right, teaching them his way" (Psalm 25:9).

My response: I love that when we humble ourselves, Lord, and admit how weak and lost we truly are, You lead us and show us what to do. Thank You for teaching me, through Your Word, the right way to go. Help me to remember Your nearness. I simply need to ask.

Additional Study Options:

What do you learn about God from Psalm 25? Add to your list in the Study Notes section at the back of this book or in your own journal.

Read All the Psalms Plan: Read Psalm 26.

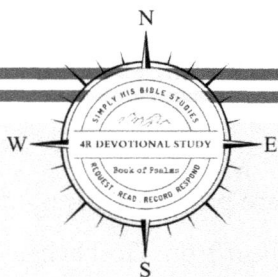

Psalm 27

Request: Dear Father, show me the path You want me to follow today as I look to You for guidance in Your Word. In Jesus' Name, Amen.

Read: Psalm 27

Record: Write down one verse from this passage that stood out to you.

Respond: Write a short prayer, talking to God about that verse.

What scares you? I think all of us have a few things we'd rather avoid. I don't like big insects that fly at my head, standing near the edge of a cliff, or snakes. It's a pretty natural part of being human to fear certain things, isn't it? In today's psalm, David is preaching himself a sermon on how to react when afraid. It's marvelous!

David was being chased down by Saul, the King of Israel. Now, when the king of the land is chasing you with intent to kill, even some of your friends keep a careful distance from you. David felt alone, surrounded, and abandoned. If he got caught, he would most likely be killed. I think he had a much better reason to fear than I do when I overreact to an insect flying at me!

So, David gives himself a pep talk, exchanging truth for the lies that fear was whispering to his heart. There are so many truths in this psalm. Right out of the gate, David declares that God is his light and his salvation. God is his fortress and protection. God is on his side. What's a king and a nation compared to that? They're all nothing. Piffle, as my British relatives would say. When we belong to Him, He is most definitely in the business of caring for us, so we don't need to fear kings or nations.

David runs to the Lord in prayer and declares how much he loves being near Him, delighting in His perfections, longing to worship in His sanctuary. One of my favorite verses in this psalm gives us a glimpse at their close relationship, David and His God: "My heart has heard you say, 'Come and talk with me.' And my heart responds, 'LORD, I am coming'" (Psalm 27:8). Isn't that beautiful? God wants us to come and talk with Him about our troubles and fears. He listens. He holds us. David eagerly comes close to Him, and as he does, his fear dissipates.

David ends this psalm with a bit of advice for us all. He tells us to "wait patiently" for God's rescue. He knows whereof he speaks. He waited at least ten years for rescue. This puts me to shame, for I am often discouraged if God doesn't answer me within minutes! Always, we can draw near to God. Always, we can remind ourselves that He is near. The rock-solid truth for Christians is that there will never be a time when He doesn't love us, whether we live or die and live again in Heaven. So, let's take courage and be brave. Let's wait with sure confidence for the Lord.

My verse: "Wait patiently for the LORD. Be brave and courageous. Yes, wait patiently for the LORD" (Psalm 27:14).

My response: It takes courage and bravery to be still and wait for You, Lord. Especially when the wait is long. Give me the deep faith that waits and knows that You, Sovereign God, will someday make it all right and good again. Lord, I wait.

Additional Study Options:

What do you learn about God from Psalm 27? Add to your list in the Study Notes section at the back of this book or in your own journal.

Read All the Psalms Plan: Read Psalm 28.

Psalm 30

Request: Here I am, Father God. Sitting with Your living Word open, eager to hear from You. Please teach me and guide me today. In Jesus' Name, Amen.

Read: Psalm 30

Record: Write down one verse from this passage that stood out to you.

Respond: Write a short prayer, talking to God about that verse.

Before I even began reading Psalm 30, I was brought up short by the title. In my Bible, the New Living Translation, it says: "A psalm of David. A song for the dedication of the Temple." That's an odd title when you remember that there was no temple during David's reign. David longed to build a temple for the LORD His God but was denied the blessing of doing so by God Himself.

Here is what God said to David through Nathan the prophet: "For when you die and are buried with your ancestors, I will raise up one of your descendants, your own offspring, and I will make his kingdom strong. He is the one who will build a house—a temple—for my name. And I will secure his royal throne forever" (2 Samuel 7:12-13).

David explains the reason for God's refusal to let him be the one to build the temple in 1 Chronicles: "David rose to his feet and said: 'My brothers and my people! It was my desire to build a Temple where the Ark of the LORD's Covenant, God's footstool, could rest permanently. I made the necessary preparations for building it, but God said to me, 'You must not build a Temple to honor my name, for you are a warrior and have shed much blood'" (1 Chronicles 28:2-3).

So, why would David write a psalm of dedication for the temple he would never see? I read different opinions given by various Bible scholars. The one that resonated the most with me is that David wrote this psalm ahead of time, in faith believing that Solomon would build the temple. I think he wanted a song sung that he had composed once it was done. That seems the most likely to me, and it definitely was the one that made me smile!

Interestingly, this psalm doesn't talk about the temple. Instead, it reminds the temple-goers that even though the path through life can be hard and difficult, eventually joy does come! David waited years to be king. But that finally happened. He longed for the building of the temple. It took place many years after his death. But it finally happened, too. David endured many trials and setbacks in his life—some of his own making. Time and again in David's life, his circumstances seemed hopeless. Yet he pours out hope in Psalm 30.

"Cheer up," David seems to be saying. There will be periods of intense grief and sadness in this life, but they will not last. A time will come when we will laugh and dance in astonished joy as God brings victory either to a personal struggle or to the larger struggle of living in a very broken world. This is a psalm of triumphant hope. It's a good one to read when hope seems very far away. Let's give Him thanks for that today!

My verse: "I cried out to you, O LORD. I begged the Lord for mercy . . . " (Psalm 30:8a).

My response: When all is going wrong and I feel the onset of despair, help me to remember to still cry out to You, asking for Your mercy. Lord God, You are always near. How I thank You that even in the worst of times I can sob out my needs and cling to You. Others may desert me, but You stay near. Thank You!

Additional Study Options:

What do you learn about God from Psalm 30? Add to your list in the Study Notes section at the back of this book or in your own journal.

Read All the Psalms Plan: Read Psalm 29.

Psalm 31

Request: Thank You, Father, for the incredible privilege of being able to meet with You, talk with You, and hear Your words in the Bible today. I don't want to ever take this for granted! Give me ears to hear You, Lord, as I open Your Word. In Jesus' Name, Amen.

Read: Psalm 31

Record: Write down one verse from this passage that stood out to you.

Respond: Write a short prayer, talking to God about that verse.

Once upon a time, when I was an awkward freshman in high school, a popular girl called me over to the crowd she hung around with. I was astounded. She was calling . . . me? I gladly went with my best smile on my face. "Sharon," she said, "I have just got to show you this. It is sooo ugly!" I prepared to look at something ugly, even though I really didn't want to. I figured I should be polite, right? So, as I bent down to look, she held a mirror up to my face. Yes, she did. I was the ugly thing she and that crowd of kids wanted me to see. How do you recover from that when you are fourteen and already feeling unattractive and unpopular?

The sting of that memorable day has long since faded, and I am very happy with how God made me these days. When I think back, I realize that this girl felt insecure herself and was trying to score points with the others. I hope she grew up into someone much nicer than the person she was that day!

Have you ever been blindsided by a friend or acquaintance? Ever been deeply wounded by someone who has totally misunderstood you? The betrayal cuts deeply, doesn't it? One feels a bit lost and unmoored. In today's psalm, David is honest about his own hurts and betrayals. He's also quite aware of his own sins and the part they may have played. I love that he feels free to run to God and tell Him all about it. I love even more that God, in His Sovereignty, enabled this song of the nation of Israel to be included in the Old Testament. It helps us to see where to go when we've been betrayed, wounded, or unfairly accused.

We run straight to the One who always loves us. The One who does not change but is faithful and true, through and through. And we pour out all the hurts and anger and mess of our emotions into His listening ears. David doesn't soften up his feelings to sound "polite" to God. Nope.

"I am dying from grief; my years are shortened by sadness. Sin has drained my strength; I am wasting away from within . . . I am ignored as if I were dead, as if I were a broken pot" (Psalm 31:10, 12). David didn't need to write a formal essay or keep to one subject at a time. He just dumped out every feeling, from joy in God's closeness to anguish in his emotional torment.

We can do this, too.

Let's turn some of today's verses into a praise prayer as we end today's commentary. We have a God who listens and cares and doesn't demand we clean up our act and speak sensibly when we are upset. He's there for us. He holds us. Let's praise:

> How great is the goodness You have stored up for those of us who fear You, God! You lavish that goodness on us when we come to You for protection. You are able to hide me in the shelter of Your Presence, safe from those who conspire against me. Thank You for the shelter You provide, far from accusing tongues. You have shown us the wonders of Your unfailing love and we praise You!

My verse: "I will be glad and rejoice in your unfailing love, for you have seen my troubles, and you care about the anguish of my soul" (Psalm 31:7).

My response: Help me, Lord, to choose gladness. To dwell on Your unfailing love. To know and trust that You see my troubles and You care about the anguish of my soul. I am never alone, Father! And You always care—even when You allow hard things. Thank You.

Additional Study Options:

What do you learn about God from Psalm 31? Add to your list in the Study Notes section at the back of this book or in your own journal.

Read All the Psalms Plan: No extra reading today.

Hopefully, by now, we are all "hitting our stride." This describes the point in a long-distance run when the runner has found a steady rhythm that feels maintainable for the foreseeable future. Is that you? I hope so. Unlike in a long-distance run, where many distractions are removed, you, dear one, are still in the thick of life. If you have little ones at home, they will inevitably need you when you wish to be in the Word. They will get sick and require your full attention . . . you get my drift. Even if you have no children at home, as is my case, there are still many interruptions that can derail a pattern. My prayer for each of you is that you continue to fight for your precious time with God, working it into your day, even if your "normal" time gets interrupted. **Spending time with God is so valuable.** Even when life is very hard, we find greater strength when we've spent time with Him and been reminded that He is with us. May He help you sit at His feet each and every day, giving you strength to meet the tasks you will face!

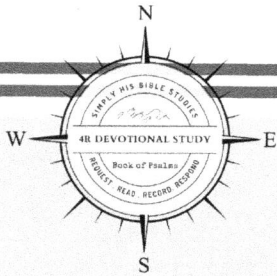

Psalm 32

Request: Heavenly Father, help me this morning to listen intently to You as I read, placing all my worries and cares in Your competent hands. Help me to focus only on what You say to me. In Jesus' Name, Amen.

Read: Psalm 32

Record: Write down one verse from this passage that stood out to you.

Respond: Write a short prayer, talking to God about that verse.

I was a determined and disciplined parent. I had read all the books and rolled up my sleeves to the task of shaping the young lives under my command into wonderful Christian adults, able to serve God fully and gladly. This rigid plan went quite well for a season. At first, I homeschooled my daughters, and then they transferred to a Christian school. I monitored what they watched and how they thought and what they wore. I couldn't see it at the time, but I was filled with a legalistic pride in "doing it right" as if children could be made to be good.

As I am sure you have guessed, things did not go according to plan. Being too strict and not truly listening to the heart of a child can be as disastrous as being too lenient. I hurt both my girls deeply through my striving for perfection, and as I realized my errors, I went through an awful time of personal upheaval. Like David in Psalm 32, I refused to confess my sins for a season. To admit that I had failed in the one area in which I had invested so deeply felt impossible and horrible.

Yet, also like David, when I finally went to God in humble repentance, confessing my sin of pride and desire to be in control, the relief was great. The healing was beautiful. And my understanding and awe of His grace grew exponentially. Confessing sin did not kill me. Refusing to confess almost did!

Confession is simply an honest conversation with God. We admit our sin and beg for His help and mercy. We express our desire to repent, turn from our sin, and do differently. Remember what happened when the prodigal son returned to his father's home, hoping he could just be a servant on the farm? Did his father scold and give him a long lecture? Was the son put on trial to see if he meant it? No and no. The father in the story ran to him, held him closely, and celebrated his return. This is what happens when we finally give in and admit our desperate need for God's help and mercy. We are held.

Don't delay if there is some besetting, ugly sin in your life of which God has made you aware. Confess it quickly. The guilt, shame, and heaviness will be washed away in a moment, and His arms will hold you tightly. Both daughters are walking with the Lord today, and I am so grateful. Believe me when I tell you that this is not because of the parenting they received. It's because of the great grace of God who sought them and called them to Himself. He answered my prayers, healed my heart, and fixed what I broke. Oh, how I praise Him! Study this psalm well and remember the lessons therein. We serve a wonderful God who guides us along the best path for our lives and gives us songs of victory when we turn to Him and confess our sins.

My verses: "Finally, I confessed my sins to you and stopped trying to hide my guilt. I said to myself, 'I will confess my rebellion to the LORD.' And you forgave me! All my guilt is gone. *Selah*" (Psalm 32:5).

My response: Oh, how foolish we humans can be, cowering in the dark, covered in shame. When we confess, You forgive and cleanse and free us! All our guilt is gone. How I praise You for this incredible, ongoing gift of forgiveness.

Additional Study Options:

What did you learn about God from Psalm 32? Add to your list in the Study Notes section at the back of this book or in your own journal.

Read All the Psalms Plan: Read Psalm 33.

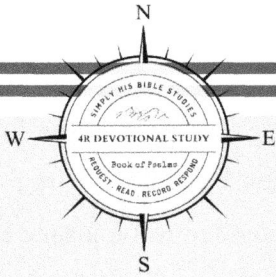

Psalm 34

Request: Oh, Father! Thank You that I get to be with You whenever I want because of Your great forgiveness and love. Thank You for wanting me close and for hearing my heart. I adore You! In Jesus' Name, Amen.

Read: Psalm 34

Record: Write down one verse from this passage that stood out to you.

Respond: Write a short prayer, talking to God about that verse.

Our psalm today was written after a specific event in David's life. If you want to read the full story, you can find it in 1 Samuel 21:10-22:1. However, you might then be confused by the inscription at the beginning of Psalm 34, which tells us that David pretended to be insane in front of Abimelech. 1 Samuel tells us David pretended to be insane in front of Achish, King of Gath. There are three possible explanations for this discrepancy. First, the inscriptions of the psalms were not part of the original text, and it could have been a mistake. Second, over and over in the Bible, the same people are given different names. Gideon, for example, was also known as Jerub-baal (Judges 6:32). Solomon was also called Jedidiah (2 Samuel 12:24, 25). Third, David could have pulled this stunt more than once in front of different kings. I'm going with explanation two or three, but I am content to wait until Heaven to ask about it. The heart of the story and the psalm remain unchanged.

What a wild story! David is hiding in Gath when he is discovered and in danger of being killed. Immediately, he acts like an insane person would, scratching on doors and drooling. That was quick thinking! Instead of being killed, he's deemed harmless and kicked out of Gath back to Israel. There he forms a band of men and starts to care for them in the wilderness while continuing to hide from Saul.

David must have worked hard on Psalm 34. It's an acrostic poem with each line beginning with a letter of the Hebrew alphabet in order. It's full of relief, praise, and thanksgiving for how God rescued him. He boasts about his great God, longing to stir up admiration for God in those around him. He urges us to "taste and see" that God is good. To experience for ourselves God's saving power and goodness to all who run to Him. This joyous psalm teaches us so much about the God David loved and served. Our God. The same One who loves us as He loved David!

What was your favorite verse in this psalm? There were so many I could have chosen. I loved the advice in the psalm that told me to find refuge in God, to keep my tongue from speaking evil, to search for peace, to look to Him. I loved David's celebration as he assures me that God is near when my heart is broken. God sees a crushed spirit, and over and over He rescues us from the many troubles that beset us in this life.

When you are facing heartbreak or extreme trouble, remember to read Psalm 34 and take hope. David had despaired for a moment in Gath when he was discovered. His only solution seemed to be to pretend insanity. He didn't want to lie about who he was, after all. It seemed hopeless. And yet, God rescued him once again. And that rescue led to our beautiful psalm of praise. No matter how many troubles we face, God is with us. Today let's celebrate that with a bit of exuberant joy of our own!

My verse: "The righteous person faces many troubles, but the LORD comes to the rescue each time" (Psalm 34:19).

My response: Dear Father, there is so much truth in these few words. The righteous—those who belong to you and who try to do good—will still have many troubles. That's the sad, plain truth. We don't magically get a perfect, care-free life when we come to You. And yet, You rescue. Every. Time. How I thank You for that rhythm to my life. Troubles come, You rescue. Over and over, I have seen Your hand at work, caring for me and mine. Thank You!

Additional Study Options:

What did you learn about God from Psalm 34? Add to your list in the Study Notes section at the back of this book or in your own journal.

Read All the Psalms Plan: Read Psalm 35.

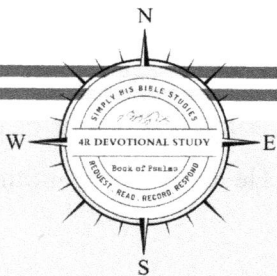

Psalm 36

Request: Heavenly Father, thank You for Your mercy, Your forgiveness, and Your welcome to all who turn to You. I'm turning to You right now, Lord. Please teach me from Your Word. In Jesus' Name, Amen.

Read: Psalm 36

Record: Write down one verse from this passage that stood out to you.

Respond: Write a short prayer, talking to God about that verse.

Psalm 36 starts with a four-verse meditation on the hearts of the wicked. Verse two especially hit me: "In their blind conceit, they cannot see how wicked they really are." Oh, how sad this is! If a person hardens her heart enough, she is no longer aware of the awful decisions she is making. Each one gets justified in her own mind, and she continues in folly. Those first four verses were depressing to read but gave great insight into the foolish blindness of a heart that has given way to evil.

I was surprised at the abrupt change from meditation to a swelling song of praise that followed. Were you? As I pondered this, I wondered if David felt like enough time had been given to thinking about evil. It was as if he shook his head to clear it and then plunged into the breathtaking goodness of God in his poetic prayer. Sometimes my mind gets stuck on a subject that is sucking me into a whirlpool of worry or despair. When that happens, the best thing I can do is what David did. Pray. Turn my heart intentionally from the unhappy thoughts to the reality of who God is and the joy of life with Him.

If you are participating in the optional assignment of listing what you learn about God from each psalm, you could fill a page with all David writes here. We go from despair to awe in a nanosecond as David praises God for His unfailing love, His faithfulness, His righteousness, His justice, and His tender care for people and animals. (Don't you just love how God cares for animals, too? This makes me smile!)

David closes this psalm beautifully. He cries out for God's justice for those who are honest. He asks for help when we encounter the evil folk bent on destruction. And, in the very last verse of this psalm-song, David declares the triumph and victory to come. God will bring justice to the earth again. Let's hear his declaration as we close out this commentary today: "Look! Those who do evil have fallen! They are thrown down, never to rise again" (Psalm 36:12). To those who have been bullied, abused, belittled, and injured deeply by evil people, this is a reassurance, indeed. It won't always be this way, dear hurting one. One day our just God will right every wrong. You can count on it.

My verses: "For you are the fountain of life, the light by which we see" (Psalm 36:9).

My response: You are the fountain of life, and You keep sending me the oxygen needed to fill my lungs. Each day I draw breath is only because of the life You pour into me! You are the light. You've revealed to me the mystery that there is life after death. I am so glad I am Yours! In Jesus' Name, Amen.

Additional Study Options:

What did you learn about God from Psalm 36? Add to your list in the Study Notes section at the back of this book or in your own journal.

Read All the Psalms Plan: Read Psalm 37.

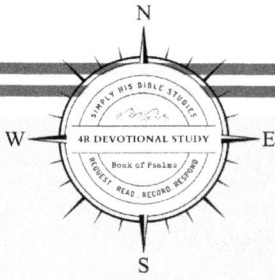

Psalm 38

Request: Lord, keep my mind focused on the good, wise, and lovely things today. Help me not to dwell on the ugly things that generate fear in me. Remind me, instead, that You are seated calmly on Your throne, managing it all just fine. Remind me that there is a very happy ending secured in advance for all who love You and are called to follow Your paths. Teach me, please. In Jesus' Name, Amen.

Read: Psalm 38

Record: Write down one verse from this passage that stood out to you.

Respond: Write a short prayer, talking to God about that verse.

David is not doing well in Psalm 38. This is a psalm of anguish, panic, anxiety, and pain. It makes me wonder how it sounded when it was sung. I also wonder how often it was sung in the temple. It must have been written in a minor key! Even though it is the song of a deeply distressed man, I suspect it resonated in many a heart. In his agony, David gives us words to say when the hurt is so deep that we don't have words of our own. Let this thought soak in for a bit: David's screaming pain was not only allowed, but these words became part of Israel's worship when they gathered. It is okay to cry out to God in anguish.

Furthermore, it is okay to cry out to God in anguish when we are to blame for our pain. Yes, David admits that he did something deeply wrong. He is gripped by fear and terror. He sees his agony and brokenness as allowed by God because of his horrendous sin. His heart beats wildly, and his strength fails as he aches over his sin and its consequences, hurting himself and others. He repents and begs God to come to him and help him. His description of this time in his life is heartrending.

On a lesser level, I have been where David was when he wrote this psalm. I've known the consequences of speaking wrathful words at someone I love. I've watched them turn away from me, hurt beyond words because of the sting and unfairness of what I said. Then my own suffering begins, as I see the pain I've caused and the chasm I've created. I can't take my words back, and their effect can last a long time. I chose anger and selfishness instead of patience and self-control, and my remorse may not instantly fix the result of my choices. I've felt the ache of knowing that something valuable broke, and I was responsible for breaking it.

Many believe this psalm was written after David's adultery with Bathsheba. David's agony was truly fierce.

So much broke on the day he lusted after Bathsheba and gave way to his own desires in spite of knowing it was sin. Oh, the consequences of his sin and the people he hurt! David blatantly disregards his lawful wives. As a result of deliberately putting Bathsheba's husband on the front line in battle where he was killed, an innocent man's death is on David's conscience. Bathsheba becomes pregnant and is forced to marry the king who caused her shame. Even David's relationships with his own children were shattered.

Yet even then, David cried out to God. This is a life lesson for all of us. No matter our sin, we can always turn back toward the God who loves us and repent. It's okay to spell out the awfulness of how we feel. It's good to declare it's our own rotten fault when it is. And it's very good to wait on God for His mercy and forgiveness. He will forgive. John assures us of this: "But if we confess our sins to him, he is faithful and just to forgive us our sins and to cleanse us from all wickedness" (1 John 1:9). Oh, how good it is to be honest and real with the Lord who sees and knows us, and still, in His mercy and grace, forgives us time and time again!

My verse: "But I confess my sins; I am deeply sorry for what I have done" (Psalm 38:18).

My response: It's only when I confess—when I name what I have done—that Your flood of forgiveness and grace pours over me and washes away my guilt and shame. As long as I do not acknowledge and name my sin, it festers and grows, disrupting my soul and my walk with You. Help me, Lord, to be quick to confess!

Additional Study Options:

What did you learn about God from Psalm 38? Add to your list in the Study Notes section at the back of this book or in your own journal.

Read All the Psalms Plan: Read Psalm 39.

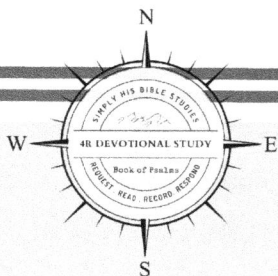

Psalm 40

Request: Thank You, Father, that You bid me come to You when all is going well, when I am deeply troubled, and even when I am ashamed. Always, You are there, ever-present God. I come near to You today with gratitude. Please teach me from Your Word. In Jesus' Name, Amen.

Read: Psalm 40

Record: Write down one verse from this passage that stood out to you.

Respond: Write a short prayer, talking to God about that verse.

It should have been the best of times. Finally, after a five-year wait, we had a precious one-year-old daughter and another baby on the way. I had longed to be a mother and struggled mightily with the delay. Here I was, living my dream. And yet, I was sunk so low in depression that even folding the laundry looked like an insurmountable task. The depression was heavy, dark, and unrelenting. The guilt I felt at not rejoicing in the answer to my many prayers made it even worse. I came close to despair the summer we moved from Alabama to Massachusetts, pregnant with my second child, and barely able to care for my firstborn.

Have you ever experienced that kind of debilitating depression? It's awful. I never had until that summer. I have been blessed with an optimistic temperament, and until that time, I had no idea what it is like to be dreadfully broken emotionally. I didn't understand how it affects one physically, mentally, and spiritually. It was good for me to feel that pit that David talks about in Psalm 40. David calls it a "pit of despair" in my translation, a place of "mud and mire." Blech. Can't you just see that deep, dark, dirty hole in the ground and a poor human stuck at the bottom?

David gives us some great insight into times of despair and depression and what to do during those times. As he opens this psalm, David declares, "I waited patiently for the LORD to help me" (Psalm 40:1a). In faith, we have to believe that these times of pit-dwelling will not last forever. There may be a season of patient endurance, but there will come a day of rescue. There will. For most of us, that comes in this life here on the earth. To all of us who belong to Him, rescue will come, even if we have to wait until Heaven. Therefore, we need not despair. David comforts us as he describes God's rescue, pulling him from the pit and steadying his feet on solid ground once again. What comfort this brings to realize David struggled, too. Furthermore, God eventually rescued him, and He will rescue us.

Hebrews 13:8 declares, "Jesus Christ is the same yesterday, today, and forever." What joy! Our God does not change. He is still the One who rescues and saves. This is evident in the great rescue Jesus initiated when He chose to die and pay the price for our sins, conquering death and despair for good. Hallelujah!

I love how David's ending to Psalm 40 is repeated in Psalm 70 (and perhaps other psalms, as well). The truth and the plea are there in both psalms: "You are my helper and my savior. O my God, do not delay" (Psalm 40:17b and Psalm 70:5b). First, there's a statement of faith spoken from the pit, declaring what is true even when not felt or seen: You are my helper and savior. Then, there comes a plea: O LORD, do not delay.

Sometimes, when I can't form words on my own, I rely on Scripture to speak for me. This short sentence might be a great one to memorize for the pit-dwelling times! I am happy to tell you that my depression eventually lifted, and I was able to enjoy being a mama to two wee ones just 15 months apart. Even though I've had ordinary times of sadness, I thank God that I've never endured such a dismal time again. I'm thankful for that window into the reality of depression as it gave me increased empathy for all who struggle with it. If you are one of them, may God be your helper and savior and lift you out of the pit without delay! And if He chooses to delay, don't despair. He sees you and will give you strength to endure even if you wait until the day He brings you home.

My verse: "He lifted me out of the pit of despair, out of the mud and the mire. He set my feet on solid ground and steadied me as I walked along" (Psalm 40:2).

My response: Lord, help me to wait patiently as David did for Your help. It will come. You will pull me from any pit of depression or trouble that comes my way. You will steady me once again. I can count on that, even if there's a time of patient waiting first. Thank You for this reminder today, Lord, that I can count on You.

Additional Study Options:

What did you learn about God from Psalm 40? Add to your list in the Study Notes section at the back of this book or in your own journal.

Read All the Psalms Plan: Read Psalm 41.

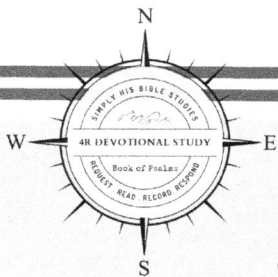

Psalms 42-43

Request: Thank You, God, for this set-apart time for just the two of us. Open my eyes to the beauty of Your Word, and show me the thought You have for me today as I seek You and Your will for my life. In Jesus' Name, Amen.

Read: Psalms 42-43

Record: Write down one verse from this passage that stood out to you.

Respond: Write a short prayer, talking to God about that verse.

I chose to have you read two psalms today because many scholars believe they are meant to be sung together. They share an identical refrain.

> Why am I discouraged?
> Why is my heart so sad?
> I will put my hope in God!
> I will praise him again—
> my Savior and my God!
> —Psalm 42:5,11 and 43:5

I wonder if, having sung that refrain in synagogue, various people over the centuries sang it to themselves mid-week when they needed to move from discouragement back to hope. I bet they did! I would love to hear this with a catchy tune for today. I think I'd like to memorize it and sing it as needed, as well.

We've entered the second book of psalms within the big book of Psalms. We're going to get to enjoy some psalm-songs written by the descendants of Korah that start to appear in the second book. If you are doing the group study, you'll be looking at greater detail at these remarkable musicians during your Week Four Group Study. Korah was a rebel during the time of Moses. God's displeasure with him was severe enough that Korah was swallowed whole by the earth itself. Yikes. And yet, centuries later, Korah's descendants humbly redeem their heritage and worship the living God, creating songs for others to sing as well. It's a wonderful redemption story.

In these two psalms, we seesaw between a yearning for God, who seems far away, and declarations of trust in Him anyway. This rock-solid faith in God is so rich and good. Hebrews 11:1 defines faith for us this way: "Now faith is confidence in what we hope for and assurance about what we do not see" (NIV). It's easier to have faith when the sun is shining and God has granted all your requests. Faith is stretched, however, and made to grow stronger when our belief that God is real and true remains even in the midst of grim circumstances. If God is real—and He is—that does not change based on our emotions or personal wishes. He is real. And that's that.

The sons of Korah help us sing this out in psalms 42 and 43. They don't ignore the pain we often feel or the yearning for a closer walk with God, especially when we know He is there but cannot see Him. These psalms lead us to praise Him anyway, to continue to talk to Him and cry out to Him with our honest thoughts and needs. I love these psalms!

One of my favorite verses is found in Psalm 42: "But each day the LORD pours his unfailing love upon me, and through each night I sing his songs, praying to God who gives me life" (Psalm 42:8). Oh, how we need to remember all the ways God shows His love to us each day despite our troubles. He gives us breath. He enables us to think and move. We would have no life apart from Him. All we are and all we do have is because He has given it. It's this kind of thinking that should fill our thoughts day and night. Let's not get so consumed by present afflictions that we forget to see that He makes the sun to shine each day and the moon to come out each night. He keeps our planet exactly the right distance from the sun so we are warmed but not burned. There are always reasons to worship and thank Him. Right in the midst of the hard. These psalms show us how.

My verse: "Day and night I have only tears for food, while my enemies continually taunt me, saying, 'Where is this God of yours?'" (Psalm 42:3).

My response: I am so thankful, Father, for this acknowledgment that there are times in life when the grief is so strong that tears are our constant companions. When a time like that comes to me, please remind me of this psalm. Help me to let the tears out but also put my hope in You as I cry. Thank You for always being near.

Additional Study Options:

What did you learn about God from Psalms 42-43? Add to your list in the Study Notes section at the back of this book or in your own journal.

Read All the Psalms Plan: No extra reading today.

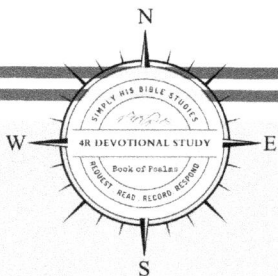

Psalm 44

Request: I'm so thankful I get to be with You, Lord, in this quiet moment. Hush my heart and help me listen, please. In Jesus' Name, Amen.

Read: Psalm 44

Record: Write down one verse from this passage that stood out to you.

Respond: Write a short prayer, talking to God about that verse.

This was a jarring psalm to read. It starts out so triumphant and happy. Our writer is thrilled with all God has done in the past for His people. He's astounded and so grateful. He gives God honor for His mighty power and proclaims that God did the saving, not the might of an army. He would wholeheartedly agree with Jesus's declaration in John 15:5b: ". . . apart from me you can do nothing" (NIV). The praises ring out in that first section, don't they?

Then, we come to an interlude or "selah" in the psalm. No one knows for sure what that Hebrew word *selah* means. Most likely, it's a musical term that calls for a pause in the song, perhaps to change the tempo or reflect and meditate on what has just been sung. In Psalm 44, the change after that directed pause is huge.

After beginning with genuine admiration and praise for all God has done and is capable of doing, the psalmist suddenly shows his anger and frustration. He is not happy with what God has allowed. This probably was written after the Assyrian invasion in 722 BC, but no one is certain. The invasions we read about in the Bible are specifically allowed by God due to the rebellion of idolatry and a turning away from the Lord. Yet, in this psalm, the writer declares the innocence of God's people in the matter.

Perhaps our psalmist really did feel like he and those in his friendship circle were innocent. They had not turned to idols and yet they were swept into the disaster along with everyone else. Do you remember being punished as a child because the majority of your classmates were mischievous even though you were not? Sometimes, the innocent are punished along with the guilty! And when that happens, our human reaction is to cry, "Not fair!" Our psalm writer is definitely feeling that unfairness, poor guy.

God alone knows if the psalmist was as innocent as he proclaimed himself to be. He certainly wasn't blameless. None of us is! Isn't it fascinating that this son of Korah felt freedom to not only remind God of what He was capable of doing but also to declare how unhappy he was that God did not help them in their catastrophe? We can go to God with all our stuff—the good, the bad, the ugly. He sees our hearts, in any case, so we might as well confess it to Him. That's what this son of Korah did. He ends with this heartfelt plea:

> We collapse in the dust,
> lying face down in the dirt.
> Rise up! Help us!
> Ransom us because of your unfailing love.
> —Psalm 44:25-26

Despite the disaster, the ruin, the feeling of loss and abandonment, he still cries out to God Most High, the only one who can ransom us because of His unfailing love. He's still the only one. And oh, how glad I am that Jesus paid that ransom for us, and we are safely held by the One who loves us!

My verse: "They did not conquer the land with their swords; it was not their own strong arm that gave them victory. It was your right hand and strong arm and the blinding light from your face that helped them, for you loved them" (Psalm 44:3).

My response: Help me to always, always acknowledge that apart from You I can do nothing. Any victory or success is only because You helped me. And You help us because You love us. Thank You, Father, for Your unfailing love.

Additional Study Options:

What did you learn about God from Psalm 44? Add to your list in the Study Notes section at the back of this book or in your own journal.

Read All the Psalms Plan: Read Psalm 45.

By now, you are well into this study, and most likely, a pattern of sorts has emerged for you. So, let's talk about daily habits for a moment. Most, if not all, of us brush our teeth each day at least once. Right? What happens if we skip a day? Hmmm . . . not a lot, especially if we suck on a breath mint. Our teeth survive the neglect, and the only noticeable difference is the need for that breath mint! If we skip a few days, our teeth start to show it. I won't describe it to you, because we'd rather not even think about it! Well, when we miss a day of time with God in the Bible, we probably won't notice much of a difference. We may have to try harder to be nice because we haven't sat with Love Himself and been filled afresh with His love. However, if we miss meeting with Him day after day, we start to be coated with selfishness, not shiny and clean, but dull. The sweet, daily habit of coming to the Lord is so cleansing! He pours out His love and His teaching, and even if we aren't aware of what He is doing in us, it matters. When we don't spend that time with Him, we see how much we need it. Keep brushing your teeth. Keep meeting with the King. It's so worth it.

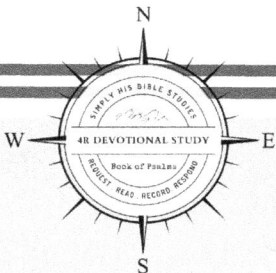

Psalm 46

Request: Father God, may this time with You never lose its awe for me. You, King of the universe, deign to be with me, ready to teach me and hold me as I come to Your Word today. Thank You for this incredible privilege. In Jesus' Name, Amen.

Read: Psalm 46

Record: Write down one verse from this passage that stood out to you.

Respond: Write a short prayer, talking to God about that verse.

This Psalm is one of my absolute favorites. I love all three sections of it, and I love that there are sections separated by that beautiful word, *Selah*. There are many opinions on what it means, but the most common is that it signifies a pause or break in the music. In this psalm, the "selah's" seem especially significant as the thoughts expressed are different in each section. Let's look at each section briefly and marvel at what we learn.

The first section has three verses in it, and it has the overarching theme that God alone is our refuge and strength. The sons of Korah, who wrote this, list all kinds of catastrophes to remind us that nothing is permanent in this world. Today we are able to see natural disasters that take place all around the globe. Tsunamis and earthquakes, volcanic eruptions and tornadoes, blizzards and hurricanes that come with very little warning and leave destruction in their wake. We are not invulnerable, no matter how rich or famous, to the capriciousness of nature and its moments of fury. Yet sitting above it all is God. He is our refuge and strength, and no matter the tempest, He is there with us in it. Therefore, we really have nothing to fear! *Selah.* Let's stop for a moment and think about that.

Our second section expands on why we have nothing to fear by taking us to God's permanent abode, Heaven. There's a river there that is so gorgeous and glorious that just to look at it brings joy, evidently! That city—the heavenly Jerusalem—cannot be moved. It is a disaster-free zone for all eternity. And that is our destination. If the mountains fall into the sea, and we with them, our mortal bodies might be destroyed, but our souls will rise. We will be clothed in immortality, and we will reside where no disaster can touch us. And just to seal the deal, we are reminded that it's the God of all Heaven's Armies who is the King! *Selah.* Just picture the security He gives in Heaven for a moment.

We come back to earth in the last section and are assured that there will come a day when wars will cease and all will be made right. God alone controls the ultimate fate of our world. That's how big He is. Our response should be awe and quiet. We need to be still and honor Him. *Selah*.

My verse: "A river brings joy to the city of our God, the sacred home of the Most High" (Psalm 46:4).

My response: I love these peeks into Heaven, Lord! I love that it's a place of beauty and joy. The "sacred home of the Most High" sounds wonderful and amazing. The solid reality of that joyous river, flowing even as I write, steadies me in this chaotic world. Thank You for this glimpse!

Additional Study Options:

What did you learn about God from Psalm 46? Add to your list in the Study Notes section at the back of this book or in your own journal.

Read All the Psalms Plan: Read Psalms 47-48.

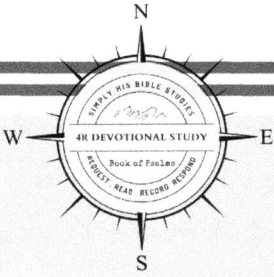

Psalm 50

Request: Oh Father, as I read this morning, I celebrate that You are my refuge and strength, an ever-present help in trouble. Be near me as I study and listen, please. In Jesus' Name, Amen.

Read: Psalm 50

Record: Write down one verse from this passage that stood out to you.

Respond: Write a short prayer, talking to God about that verse.

_____

_____

_____

_____

_____

_____

_____

_____

I was struck by God's call to thankfulness in this psalm. God urges His people to "make thankfulness your sacrifice to God" (vs. 14). He reiterates that thought later: "But giving thanks is a sacrifice that truly honors me" (vs. 23). Thankfulness matters a lot to God. There are, of course, other places in Scripture that underscore this truth. When Jesus healed ten lepers, only one returned to give Him thanks—and Jesus noticed that (Luke 17:11-19).

Before we dive deep into thankfulness, though, let's look at what did not please God. This psalm reminds us of the beauty and majesty of God. It then bemoans the fact that people can keep up with all the religious rituals—in those days, the elaborate systems of sacrifice—and yet their hearts remain far from Him. God notices that, too. He is not interested in our outside pretenses at all. He wants our hearts to be purely devoted to Him. Isn't that the desire of any lover? I don't want my husband Ray to provide for me and buy me gifts out of duty. What makes the provision and the gifts special is the love that accompanies them. Ray cares for me, and it shows not only in his actions but in how he puts up with me at times. I want Ray's heart to be soft toward me. He's my one and only guy. No gift would make up for living with a man who had no caring heart toward me. That would be so sad.

In the same way, God doesn't want people to "go through the motions." He wants us to genuinely love and notice Him. One of the ways we do that is through our gratitude. There are so many reasons to be grateful if we but take the time to look. Here are just a few . . .

. . . Most mornings, God paints the sky for us in soft pastels and brilliant hues. He didn't have to make the world beautiful, but it is! I see some of the dystopian movies where the earth is blackened, nothing green grows and everything is dull and colorless. It is terrifying! That is not the world God made for us. *His* world is gorgeous. And each day begins and ends with a sky that proclaims His glory. Are we thankful for that?

. . . Most days, we wake up and breathe freely. Our bodies function. Our minds kick into gear, and we remember what we are supposed to do that day. To not be able to experience these is a tragedy. Are we thankful for breath, for movement, for the capacity to think and wonder?

. . . If you are reading this, then you have some leisure time in your life, as I have to write it. We are not fleeing for our lives with the clothes on our backs, possessions gone, and no time to stop—just running. Are we grateful for the quiet spaces in our days that are free from terror?

Oh, there's so much that we take for granted! Thankfulness, when we are in a time of trouble, can be a sacrifice. It can be hard to look for what He is doing when all we can see is what He has not done. But gratitude will not only please Him. It will help us, too. That's the way God works. What He asks of us is not just because it is His due. It also blesses us. That's how Love works.

My verse: "I know every bird on the mountains, and all the animals of the field are mine" (Psalm 50:11).

My response: It's mind-boggling enough that You know every human, Lord. And here I'm told you know every bird! "Not a sparrow falls . . ." God of all creation, how glorious are all Your works! How marvelous You are—beyond my comprehension, worthy of my adoration.

Additional Study Options:

What did you learn about God from Psalm 50? Add to your list in the Study Notes section at the back of this book or in your own journal.

Read All the Psalms Plan: Read Psalm 49.

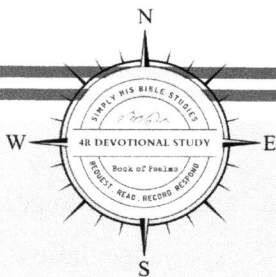

Psalm 51

Request: Here I am, Lord. Give me listening ears as I open and read Your Word, please. In Jesus' Name, Amen.

Read: Psalm 51

Record: Write down one verse from this passage that stood out to you.

Respond: Write a short prayer, talking to God about that verse.

If ever a man needed to repent, it was David. His terrible sin of lust led to adultery, murder, and even the death of a little baby. If ever we doubt God's unlimited forgiveness, we never have to look further than this story. David repented, and God indeed forgave him. He removed the heavy weight of guilt and shame from David's shoulders and restored him to fellowship.

In my opinion, the key verse to this psalm is verse 17: "The sacrifice you desire is a broken spirit. You will not reject a broken and repentant heart, O God" (Psalm 51:17). When we are completely broken by our sin, God is able to move in and cleanse, redeem, and restore. It's not when we hide our sins or minimize them. No. It's when we acknowledge and confess them, holding nothing back, that we show true repentance. This verse is very clear. God accepts and forgives the one who comes to Him for forgiveness.

Why is it so hard to repent and confess? Our pride makes it difficult for us to admit our sin, so we stuff it and may even justify it. Then it festers like a wound that has not been cleaned out. It is with us day and night, dogging our steps, reminding us of our unworthiness, mocking our pretenses, and torturing our minds.

David described the torment of unconfessed sin in an earlier psalm that we read. Psalm 38 may have been written after David's sin with Bathsheba and subsequent murder of her husband. "My guilt overwhelms me—it is a burden too heavy to bear. My wounds fester and stink because of my foolish sins . . . I am exhausted and completely crushed. My groans come from an anguished heart" (Psalm 38:3-4, 8).

If you are suffering from a hidden sin, take heart. God's compassion is great. His love is unfailing. He waits for you to come to Him with a contrite heart so that He can forgive, cleanse, and enable you to start fresh again. Don't let the enemy of your soul keep you bound by something you did in the past. Break free by confessing it to God, knowing that the One who made you is waiting for you to turn to Him so He can forgive. Once you are forgiven, unhampered by feelings of guilt and shame, you are able to hear Him more clearly. You are ready to serve Him again with joy and humility wherever He leads you. Let's not waste precious time hiding from God. Let's confess quickly and then serve Him gladly once more! How I praise our merciful God for His compassions that never fail.

My verse: "The sacrifice you desire is a broken spirit. You will not reject a broken and repentant heart, O God" (Psalm 51:17).

My response: I'm so glad that You are kind to the broken-hearted. Your mercies are new every morning, Lord. This humbles me and fills me with gratitude.

Additional Study Options:

What did you learn about God from Psalm 51? Add to your list in the Study Notes section at the back of this book or in your own journal.

Read All the Psalms Plan: Read Psalms 52-53.

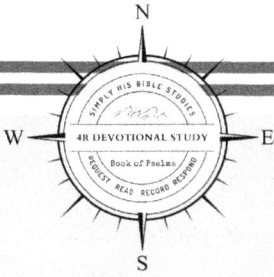

Psalm 55

Request: Father, how thankful I am that I can always come to You, no matter what I've done, and You will hear me, love me, and forgive me. There is none like You! Please teach me as I open Your Word. In Jesus' Name, Amen.

Read: Psalm 55

Record: Write down one verse from this passage that stood out to you.

Respond: Write a short prayer, talking to God about that verse.

The worst betrayals are the ones done to us by friends, aren't they? In today's psalm, David is referring to a time when he was betrayed by someone close to him. He mourns the fact that this friend used to worship with him, walking with him to the house of God. This wasn't just a friend from his old neighborhood. This was a friend who pretended to love God as David did. David feels blindsided. It's not just the hurt of the betrayal. David never thought his friend would do such a thing. Has this ever happened to you?

A long time ago, my husband and I attended a church that had an amazing preacher. This pastor convinced Ray to do things that I never could persuade him to do. You see, I grew up in a Christian home where church was a three-times-a-week happening. If the doors were open, my family would be there. My parents actually helped start that church. I came into our marriage with some core beliefs that my husband, a convert to Christianity in his late teens, did not share. Because of the powerful words and Bible exposition of this preacher, Ray decided we should tithe our income. He realized he needed to attend church weekly, not just when it was convenient. Being a Baptist church, Ray chose to be baptized as an adult. Wow. I was thrilled with Ray's newfound fervor and strengthened beliefs!

Shortly after this, we changed churches. We had become friends with another couple who attended a church right up the road from us and chose to attend there instead, bringing with us the good teaching we had received at the prior church. We missed the dynamic preaching but not the half hour drive to church each week.

Imagine our horror when we heard that the pastor we had so admired . . . the very one who had convicted my husband to draw closer to the Lord and to walk in greater obedience . . . was asked to leave the church because he had made up his resume. He had not graduated from Harvard.

He did not have a degree in psychology. The list went on and on. He had fabricated his background, and no one had checked to verify it when he was hired. This could have derailed our faith, but it did not, thanks be to God. The teaching we received that was Bible-based was still true. The man who shared it was flawed but not the principles from the Bible. We survived that upheaval, but it hurt.

When you are betrayed by someone you once trusted, don't confuse them with the always trustworthy God you love and serve. Take David's admonition in Psalm 55 to heart. "Give your burdens to the LORD, and he will take care of you. He will not permit the godly to slip and fall" (Psalm 55:22). Stay true to Him. Pray for the one who betrayed you, that he or she will repent. Remember that the Lord Jesus understands betrayal all too well, and He is able to comfort you. And keep running to God with every need, knowing He is faithful forever.

My verse: "Morning, noon, and night I cry out in my distress, and the LORD hears my voice" (Psalm 55:17).

My response: Lord, I love this rhythm of crying out to you three times each day. I love that we can come to You over and over and over. You want to hear from us!

Additional Study Options:

What did you learn about God from Psalm 55? Add to your list in the Study Notes section at the back of this book or in your own journal.

Read All the Psalms Plan: Read Psalm 54.

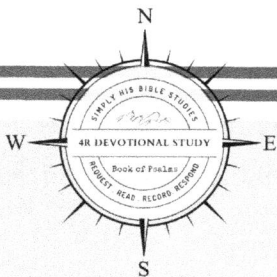

Psalm 56

Request: I come to You, Lord, desiring to hear Your good voice today. Please direct my path. In Jesus' Name, Amen.

Read: Psalm 56

Record: Write down one verse from this passage that stood out to you.

Respond: Write a short prayer, talking to God about that verse.

There's a worship song that has a line in it I often remember when I am giving way to fear. "Fear is a liar," declares the singer. This is a great truth to remember. There are two kinds of fear in the Bible: the fear of God, a deep respect and awe, and then all other fears, which are a waste of time. Jesus talks to us about that first fear in Matthew 10: "Don't be afraid of those who want to kill your body; they cannot touch your soul. Fear only God, who can destroy both soul and body in hell" (Matthew 10:28). Nothing can touch us if God is our God. Eternity is ours with Him. And nothing can save us if God is not our God, for He can destroy not only our bodies but our souls.

Once we are His, we are safe and secure. Our relief and awe should be great. The great God who holds our lives and eternal souls in His mighty hand has saved us and called us His own. He never breaks His promises, so we can rest in that.

However, the devil loves to use fear to torment us. John puts it this way in 1 John: "There is no fear in love. But perfect love drives out fear, because fear has to do with punishment. The one who fears is not made perfect in love" (1 John 4:18 NIV). Fear lies to us about the future. Let's remember that and not fall for the devil's tricks. For example, we might be given a cancer diagnosis. Fear would cause us to believe that we will be in constant pain and misery before dying in agony without peace. If we let it, fear would even steal the joy from our good days, making every day a bad day.

I have often found that the fear of an event or circumstance is worse than the event itself. If I give myself to God and cling tightly to His hand, I am amazed at not only the peace that passes understanding but the joy that comes, as well! Let's not give way to fear. God keeps track of all our sorrows and even saves up our tears. He will not allow our pain to go unnoticed or redeemed. In fact, circling back to 1 John 4:18, notice what drives out fear: God's perfect love.

When we are secure in His love, we can rest in the knowledge that God is trustworthy. If we are His, life will end well for us as we begin eternity with Him! Let's walk in His life-giving light and allow that light, as well as His perfect love, to drive out the darkness of fear. We don't have to live in fear. May God help us cling to this truth even in the darkest of times!

My verse: "But when I am afraid, I will put my trust in you" (Psalm 56:3).

My response: I love this simple verse—a prescription of sorts. When I fear, I need to take it to You, Lord, and trust You with the situation. Always, always, You draw me closer. Come near, You say! Thank You for loving me, wanting me close and unafraid.

Additional Study Options:

What did you learn about God from Psalm 56? Add to your list in the Study Notes section at the back of this book or in your own journal.

Read All the Psalms Plan: Read Psalm 57-58.

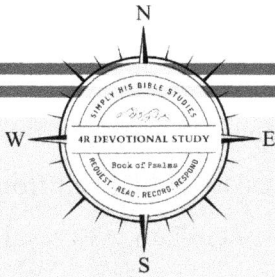

Psalm 59

Request: Thank You, Lord, for this safe and quiet space where I meet with You each day. Please teach me as I nestle in to learn. In Jesus' Name, Amen.

Read: Psalm 59

Record: Write down one verse from this passage that stood out to you.

Respond: Write a short prayer, talking to God about that verse.

_____

_____

_____

_____

_____

_____

_____

The psalms are not written in chronological order. In Psalm 51, we read about David's grief over his sin with Bathsheba. Now, a few psalms later, we read David's response to an incident from when he was very young, perhaps still in his late teens. David had just killed Goliath. As a result, he had gained King Saul's daughter Michal as his wife. He was a loyal soldier in Saul's army and his enthusiasm and courage inspired all around him. The victories were massive and his charisma made him a favorite among the soldiers. David was riding high on success. Sadly, instead of being happy for his son-in-law, Saul became treacherously jealous.

Saul had instructed his men to kill David when he walked out of his house in the morning, so David had to flee for his life in the night. What a shameful thing to ask of soldiers! To kill a defenseless man as he was leaving his home to go to work for the king! David's wife Michal got word of the plot and was able to sneak him out through a window. She lied and told the men that David was sick. They believed her for a short while before Saul sent them back to get David out of his "sickbed." That's when they discovered he had escaped. (You can read more about this in 1 Samuel 19.)

David dealt with a lot of treachery, didn't he? Can you imagine him lying in bed, knowing people were outside just waiting to kill him? Can you picture David's hurt and confusion? He had done nothing wrong. Imagine his agony as he climbed out the window and then quietly ran for his life. He left a life behind him, too. Saul made Michal marry someone else. David left the army he'd served in faithfully. He left his best friends, his brothers and father. All because of a raging, unstable king.

And, as usual, David brings all his emotions to the God he still trusts. He models for us how to be real with the One who sees everything. He cries out for protection. He points out his trouble and his innocence. He ends with the most beautiful words. God is his refuge and his strength. God rescued him in the past and will rescue him still. What a beautiful way to end this psalm! Oh, how good it is to trust in the Lord, even in the hardest of times!

My verse: "O my Strength, to you I sing praises, for you, O God, are my refuge, the God who shows me unfailing love" (Psalm 59:17).

My response: Lord, You are my Strength, too! I'm so thankful that You can help me, when I am weak, with a supernatural strength not my own. You also provide refuge. I can rest in Your unfailing love. I love being Your child.

Additional Study Options:

What did you learn about God from Psalm 59? Add to your list in the Study Notes section at the back of this book or in your own journal.

Read All the Psalms Plan: Read Psalm 60-61.

.

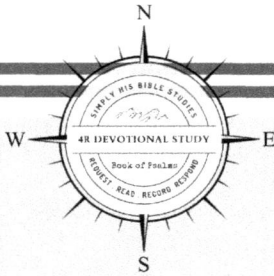

Psalm 62

Request: Holy God, I am so thankful for the intimacy You not only allow, but want . . . *with me.* Thank You for being near as I open Your Word to hear from You. In Jesus' Name, Amen.

Read: Psalm 62

Record: Write down one verse from this passage that stood out to you.

Respond: Write a short prayer, talking to God about that verse.

"Let all that I am wait quietly before God, for my hope is in him" (Psalm 62:5). As I read this psalm, verse 5 seemed to be the linchpin verse. David wrote Psalm 62 for a choir director named Jeduthun. So, this particular psalm was written for people to sing, and I find it so instructional. It's all about the wait. We often pray for victory and answers without immediate results. God frequently asks us to wait on things despite our intense desire to have them solved right away. Waiting is hard.

Let's unpack this verse as a microcosm of this psalm as a whole. David asks for help in waiting. "Let all that I am wait . . ." is his prayer. We can talk about waiting, but to have every part of our body—mind, spirit, soul, flesh—truly relaxed as we wait is almost impossible without the help of God. Yet that's what we need to do after we've made our request to Him. Settle in and wait for the answer, trusting that it will come.

The next word after wait is "quietly." This is how we should wait. I am terrible at this! If Ray is late coming home from work, I'm often pacing and looking out the window every ten seconds, wondering if I should call him. This is not a sign of trust. It's a sign of anxiety and a lack of faith. To wait quietly is to place the outcome thoroughly into God's hands. It is to believe that no matter what God decides ought to happen, it will ultimately be for our good and for the good of His kingdom. It's to entrust our desires into His good hands and to want His will above our own. When we have quieted our souls and are willing to accept His will, then the wait is sweet. We know He will move in His time for the best good.

How can we believe this? As David says in the last part of this verse, "my hope is in him." Although the days on earth surely can seem

long at times, eternity stretches forever. What we do *here*, prepares us for the much longer *there*. Our hope is not on earthly things, nice though they may be. Our hope is in Him. God alone can save our souls, clothe us with immortality, and bring us into His glorious kingdom of light! Remembering what matters eternally can help us deal with our waiting in the here and now.

Of course, there's much more to this beautiful psalm than just the waiting part. Perhaps God had you meditating on another section. How I wish you and I could sit down together and examine the verses one at a time, sharing our insights and marveling at the wisdom packed into this song. I love the richness of His Word. I hope He spoke to you in some very special way today! It's what I pray for as I write this study.

My verse: "Let all that I am wait quietly before God, for my hope is in him" (Psalm 62:5).

My response: Waiting is hard, Lord! Help me in the waiting times to wait well. With all of me. Just waiting while entrusting myself to Your plan over any plans of my own.

Additional Study Options:

What did you learn about God from Psalm 62? Add to your list in the Study Notes section at the back of this book or in your own journal.

Read All the Psalms Plan: Read Psalms 63-64.

This is our middle week of the study. How are you doing? Are you seeing repetition of thoughts and praises? I hope so. A whole lot of the Bible is repetition, and the psalms are no exception. I am never tired of hearing Ray tell me he loves me. That's a repetition that just warms my heart and assures my soul. Reading truths from God's Word imprints them on our hearts and minds and keeps us safe from the enemy, who does not want us to remember God's Word. We are weak, like "dust" that is here today and gone tomorrow. God knows this. And so He repeats and reminds and reassures throughout the Bible. Paul confirms this in his letter to the Philippians, when he repeats himself: "Whatever happens, my dear brothers and sisters, rejoice in the Lord. *I never get tired of telling you these things, and I do it to safeguard your faith*" (Philippians 3:1, emphasis mine).

This repetition is literally a safeguard for us. We read these psalms with their reminders to turn to God and we are protected from the arrows of the enemy. Jesus, when he was tempted in the desert, fought back with Scripture. Every. Time. Paul tells us in Ephesians 6 that the Bible is a sword with which we can attack the enemy. Let's wield that sword when we are attacked by immersing ourselves, day after day, in the truths found in God's Word! That is what will help us to stand firm in the days of persecution and trial.

Do you see? You are putting on your armor and suiting up each and every day you open the Bible and whisper "teach me, please." Oh, friend! We will not know completely this side of Heaven the victories that were won simply because we came faithfully each day to God's Word. Keep on keeping on!

Psalm 65

Request: Father, teach me, please. I wait on You. In Jesus' Name, Amen.

Read: Psalm 65

Record: Write down one verse from this passage that stood out to you.

Respond: Write a short prayer, talking to God about that verse.

David, in this psalm, is just full of "WOW" for God, isn't he? He's amazed and humbled that God forgives our sins. He's in awe of the beauty of God's creation. He's astounded by the vastness of the earth and how God fills every single part with His presence. He's rejoicing at the beauty of an abundant harvest after a beautiful growing season with sufficient sun and rain. This is a happy psalm!

I have a very organized prayer life. I like the way it's set up with different days set aside for different needs. I pray for my family on Mondays, including aunts, uncles and cousins all in a set pattern. I focus on unsaved friends and family on Tuesdays. Wednesdays find me praying for my husband's job as a Christian school teacher and mine as the Director of Sweet Selah Ministries. But on Thursdays? I just stop and "notice." Thanksgiving fills my prayers. That training of my mind to see all God has given has helped me to be a happier, more grateful person. There are so many wonderful things to be grateful for if we would but look around.

That's just what David does in this psalm. He helps us to be grateful. Want to try this practice of gratitude? I'll keep my commentary short today. If you have time, after you write your verse and prayer, list some thanksgivings in the back section of this book or in your journal. Take time to notice what God has done. I think you'll be amazed and delighted. Just like David.

My verses: "Those who live at the ends of the earth stand in awe of your wonders. From where the sun rises to where it sets, you inspire shouts of joy" (Psalm 65:8).

My response: This whole psalm, Lord, is a mighty shout to You—magnificent, all-powerful Savior! Your works point to Your Majesty, and You truly do inspire shouts of joy all across our planet. Thank You, Lord, for so many good gifts. This psalm made me so happy!

Additional Study Options:

What did you learn about God from Psalm 65? Add to your list in the Study Notes section at the back of this book or in your own journal.

Read All the Psalms Plan: Read Psalms 66, 67.

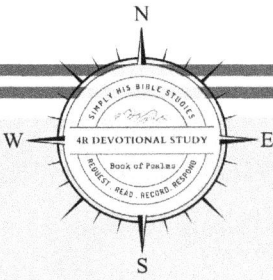

Psalm 68

Request: Father, teach me and show me the verse that You want me to meditate upon today. I believe Your Word is a living letter to me and to all who read it. Show me exactly what I need to see as I come to You with an open heart. In Jesus' Name, Amen.

Read: Psalm 68

Record: Write down one verse from this passage that stood out to you.

Respond: Write a short prayer, talking to God about that verse.

As I read this psalm in order to write my commentary, I was struck by the many themes in it. This psalm ranges from recalling Israel's history to prophecy about when God will dwell with us. In between, we read comforting words about how He treats the needy and scathing words about the decimation of God's enemies. It's a lot.

I love it when David recalls what God has done in the past. We must never forget what God has done. The Israelites often looked back to their captivity in Egypt and rescue from slavery. They remembered how God brought about the great exodus of over a million people from Egypt. They reminisced about when they left carrying jewelry and spoils given to them by Egyptians anxious for them to go. They brought to mind how God fed them with manna from Heaven. It's still astounding to this day. As Christians, we look back and never forget the rescue from sin and death that Jesus gave to us when His body was broken and His blood was willingly poured out on our behalf. Oh, may communion never grow old to us! Let's always remember the God who saves!

I love that David looks forward, too, to a time when God will vanquish enemies and live among us. "When you ascended to the heights, you led a crowd of captives. You received gifts from the people, even from those who rebelled against you. Now the LORD God will live among us there" (Psalm 68:18). If we take a peek into Revelation, John's incredible description of the time to come, we hear the echo of this thought from David. "And I heard a loud voice from the throne saying, 'Look! God's dwelling place is now among the people, and he will dwell with them. They will be his people, and God himself will be with them and be their God'" (Revelation 21:3 NIV). Someday God will dwell with us! We will see Him seated on the throne. Doesn't it make your heart yearn?

The parts about smashing the enemy are never my favorites. I am the woman who sometimes actually apologizes to insects in the house when I have to kill them. However, I have to remember that if I saw vicious people hurting—on purpose—innocent children and others without cause, I would want them stopped. Stopped. That's how I think of this. Of course we don't want people to continue torturing and mistreating the least among us. Of course we don't want invasions of peaceful villages where rape and indiscriminate torture occurs. In that light, I can understand how David, a man of war, would want to see those people . . . dead. Unable to hurt anyone anymore. Of course I want them to repent and be saved, but if they are not going to turn to God, then they simply need to be stopped. That's how I process these passages about the enemy.

Let's end with some celebrating, shall we? God is a Father to all of us but especially to those who are fatherless. How beautiful that is! He's a defender of widows and a rescuer of those who have been imprisoned. He is the Savior who carries us in His arms. And if you ever struggle with flying in airplanes, remember that He "rides on the clouds" (vs. 4) and "rides across the ancient heavens" (vs. 33). We are just as safe in the sky as we are on the ground. God's there, too.

I wonder what verse you chose from all of these. I've read the psalms many times, and God shows me something new over and over again. His Word truly is living and active, and I pray He spoke to you today as you sat and listened.

My verse: "Praise the Lord; praise God our savior! For each day he carries us in his arms" (Psalm 68:19).

My response: Lord, sometimes the future looks so frightening to me, and right now, this little verse comforts me and reminds me that You are my Savior. Each day You will carry me. Help me not to borrow tomorrow's troubles. Help me to just be happily held—today.

Additional Study Options:

What did you learn about God from Psalm 68? Add to your list in the Study Notes section at the back of this book or in your own journal.

Read All the Psalms Plan: Read Psalm 69.

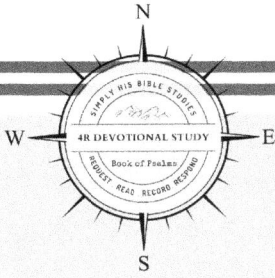

N
W E
S

SIMPLY HIS BIBLE STUDIES
4R DEVOTIONAL STUDY
Book of Psalms
REQUEST READ RECORD RESPOND

Psalm 71

Request: Dear Lord, open my eyes to see the beauty of Your written, living Word today. I'm here. I'm watching for You. In Jesus' Name, Amen.

Read: Psalm 71

Record: Write down one verse from this passage that stood out to you.

Respond: Write a short prayer, talking to God about that verse.

We don't have dates on these psalms to know exactly when they were written, but David gives us some clues in Psalm 71 that this particular song was written when he was old. How do you feel knowing that David is still struggling in old age? Do you, like me, somehow think that once you get to a certain age, you ought to be exempt from enemies and trouble? No. That's not the way it often goes.

I can remember being in my early thirties enjoying a conversation with my aunt. She'd been through a tumultuous divorce and was now happily remarried. However, she was struggling in one area of her life and shared with me how much God was teaching her as a wife. She was probably younger than I am now. I was shocked at the time. Somehow, I had thought that surely by the time I was in my fifties, I'd have conquered my anger and become a sweet, lovely person all the time. My aunt was such a beautiful and godly woman, and yet here she was openly confessing a struggle. It was a bit discouraging. I smile, now, as I think about it. All our lives, as long as we live on this broken planet and are still capable of sin, we will have troubles of many kinds.

Here's the part that gets better, though. David expresses this well in Psalm 71. The longer we walk with God, the more experiences we have had with Him helping us, guiding us, and rescuing us. We are more confident of His help because we've seen Him save us time and time again. There's a joy in running to Him in confidence that He will meet our need or give us the strength to endure whatever He has allowed. David declares with joy in verse 7, "My life is an example to many, because you have been my strength and protection" (Psalm 71:7). He can look back again and again to the many ways God has protected him.

David reminds God of this and then asks God to keep on helping even in his old age. And right after that thought, he's back to rejoicing that God will, indeed, help him. "You have allowed me to suffer much hardship, but you will restore me to life again and lift me up from the depths of the earth" (Psalm 71:20). Oh, how I hope that no matter the crises that may still be ahead of me, I continue to be like David and put my hope and trust in God. I want to run to Him in every storm, knowing that, ultimately, I will be lifted out of my mortal body and into His loving arms! The longer we serve Him, the more we know we can trust Him! Hallelujah!

My verse: "You have allowed me to suffer much hardship, but you will restore me to life again and lift me up from the depths of the earth" (Psalm 71:20).

My response: You do allow suffering and hardship, Lord. No one escapes troubles. And yet, You are there in the mess—Your Big Hand holding ours, restoring and rescuing us. I would not want to walk through life without You. You bring good from the hardships. Your closeness is such a precious, priceless gift.

Additional Study Options:

What did you learn about God from Psalm 71? Add to your list in the Study Notes section at the back of this book or in your own journal.

Read All the Psalms Plan: Read Psalm 70.

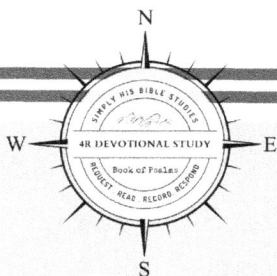

Psalm 72

Request: Here I am, Lord. Empty me of selfish thoughts and prideful ways. Help me to listen and learn as I read this morning. In Jesus' Name, Amen.

Read: Psalm 72

Record: Write down one verse from this passage that stood out to you.

Respond: Write a short prayer, talking to God about that verse.

Psalm 72 is unique in that there's a bit of controversy over its author. It's titled, "A psalm of Solomon," and yet verse 20 states, "(This ends the prayers of David son of Jesse.)" Here are a couple of different thoughts on this. First and most likely, Solomon did, indeed, write this psalm, yearning to be a good king. The parenthesis at the end might indicate that Solomon curated his dad's psalms for Book 2 of the Psalms, and this was the last psalm in that series. The second, and less likely thought, is that David wrote Psalm 72 in his last days, praying for his son Solomon as he ascended the throne. It's a bit confusing, but no worries. What really matters is the psalm itself, inspired by God and put there on purpose.

Regardless of who wrote this psalm, isn't it a beautiful prayer for a leader of a land to pray? Don't we want our leaders to behave like Solomon aspired to behave? I pray for the leaders of our country on Saturdays. I think it would be great to use some of these verses to pray for them as they make the decisions that affect those who live here. Here are some examples of how we could pray for our own leaders:

Vs. 1: Father, give our leaders Your love for justice as they make decisions.

Vs. 2: Help our courts judge rightly, and may they treat poor people fairly.

Vs. 4: Raise up defense attorneys who will genuinely defend the poor, rescuing the children of the needy, and crushing their oppressors. Help our nation's President support this.

Vs. 5: Lord, bring our leaders to repentance. "May they fear you as long as the sun shines, as long as the moon remains in the sky. Yes, forever!" (Psalm 72:5)

These are high and worthy goals for anyone who is in charge of a group of people and responsible for their welfare. Solomon started out so well, seeking God as he began his reign. I love these beautiful words found in 1 Kings that Solomon prayed as his reign began:

"Now, O Lord my God, you have made me king instead of my father, David, but I am like a little child who doesn't know his way around. And here I am in the midst of your own chosen people, a nation so great and numerous they cannot be counted! Give me an understanding heart so that I can govern your people well and know the difference between right and wrong. For who by himself is able to govern this great people of yours?"
—1 Kings 3:7-10

What humility! God can work with a man who humbly asks for help. Solomon's reign was a reign of peace and prosperity and will always be remembered by the people of Israel. Sadly, however, Solomon walked away from humility and was led astray by his many, many wives. He did not listen to God in the end, leading to a divided kingdom and much loss and heartache. Solomon started well and ended poorly. Let's not do that, okay? Let's pray that God will keep us faithful to the end. Let's ask Him to help us to love Him more and more, willing to be humbled whenever He shows us a sinful behavior that needs to be crushed. I want that so much! How about you?

As we look at this psalm, we can also see hints of the final King of kings in it. Jesus will reign with justice. He will look after the needs of the poor and destitute. He will bless us someday with a newly restored earth, beautiful beyond description! Jesus can do what no earthly leaders can do, despite their best intentions. Let's rejoice in that today!

My verse: "Long live the king! May the gold of Sheba be given to him. May the people always pray for him and bless him all day long" (Psalm 72:15).

My response: Father, in Old Testament and New, we're told to pray for our country's leaders. Help me to be faithful in this, and please raise up good and wise leaders here in the United States!

Additional Study Options:

What did you learn about God from Psalm 72? Add to your list in the Study Notes section at the back of this book or in your own journal.

Read All the Psalms Plan: No extra reading today.

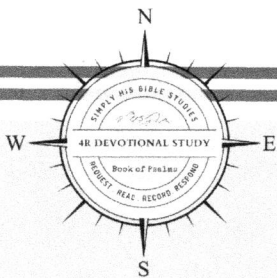

Psalm 73

Request: Lord, as I read about the king being kind and a defender of the poor yesterday, help me to also be kind and a defender of the poor. Thank You that You care for the least valued ones. Help me, too, to care. And please teach me how to live out what You are showing me as I read again today. In Jesus' Name, Amen.

Read: Psalm 73

Record: Write down one verse from this passage that stood out to you.

Respond: Write a short prayer, talking to God about that verse.

We are now going to read a series of psalms written by a prophet named Asaph. Asaph wrote 12 psalms, and 11 out of the 12 are in Book Three of the Psalms. In fact, they're all in a row: Psalms 73-83. Not all Asaph's psalms are happy ones. He is real and honest about his feelings, and we get to learn more about how to express our own feelings by reading how Asaph processes his.

As a prophet, Asaph occasionally sees into the future. He sees terrible things, and it grieves him. He was one of David's song leaders long before Jerusalem was ransacked and destroyed. Asaph "sees" these future events and laments those dark days to come in a couple of his psalms. You can learn more about him if you look at our Leader's Guide for Group Studies, Week Five.

In our psalm for today, we find Asaph puzzling over a situation that is all too common. From his perspective, the bad guys are winning. He's fallen into the trap of comparing his life to others' lives. Never a good idea. He observes that those who are rich at the expense of the poor, accumulating wealth with a total disregard for others, seem to be doing just fine. Better than fine. They're enjoying parties, jetting about on their camels and chariots, and sporting the latest garb. Asaph does not think this is fair. "Did I keep my heart pure for nothing?" (Psalm 73:13)

Have you ever been frustrated that "being good" was not rewarded as you thought it ought to have been? It can be quite frustrating, can't it? I remember vividly a situation that happened to me in seventh grade. I was taking a math test and finding it hard. I sighed. I looked up and, without meaning to, saw the answer to the problem I was on at the desk to my left. A panic inside my brain ensued. I didn't mean to look!! But now I knew the answer. But maybe I would have come to that answer anyway. What should I do? I wrote it down, finished the test, and when I brought it to the teacher told her what happened. I expected the teacher to commend me for my honesty, and perhaps just mark that one problem wrong. That is not what happened. She tore up the entire test in front of me and the class and told me I had a zero. What? I was so humiliated and angry! This was my reward for honesty? Why had I bothered?

But then, like Asaph, I was reminded by the Lord that He saw my heart and was pleased with what I had done. It was the first of many lessons in my life when I was challenged to get out of the habit of thinking life with God would be transactional. If I did this good thing, He would reward me with that good thing. Nope. If I did good things, He would be pleased with me and show me so in many beautiful ways. However, He would not suddenly make my life easy or give me all the stuff. God loves me despite the fact that I have done bad things. I ought to be extremely thankful that our relationship is not transactional!

I walk with God because He is God. He is real. He is love. He is the only way. He knows me inside and out and loves me so much He died for me so that I could live with Him forever. No matter what happens to me on earth, whether I prosper or starve, He is still God. He is still real. He still loves me and will bring me home someday. Sometimes He asks me to accept hard things. I am not to look at what others have. Nope. I simply need to walk the path marked out for me.

Don't you love Asaph's beautiful conclusion to his jealousy of the perceived ease of the rich? Asaph remembers the final destination of those who are evil. They only "win" for a very short season. Even during that short season, they also have broken relationships, sickness, disease, and regrets. It only looks good from a distance, doesn't it? Let's conclude with Asaph that we can rejoice because

God still holds our hand, guides us with His good counsel, and is leading us toward a glorious destiny! Let's serve Him because we love the One who loved us first. The transaction that mattered—Jesus taking our sins on Himself—is done. Now we walk in love with Him. That is all.

My verse: "My health may fail, and my spirit may grow weak, but God remains the strength of my heart; he is mine forever" (Psalm 73:26).

My response: No one loves me like You do, Lord, nor ever will. No matter what, because of Your great faithfulness, I am Yours and You are mine forever! I rejoice in this, Lord, and I worship You.

Additional Study Options:

What did you learn about God from Psalm 73? Add to your list in the Study Notes section at the back of this book or in your own journal.

Read All the Psalms Plan: No extra reading today.

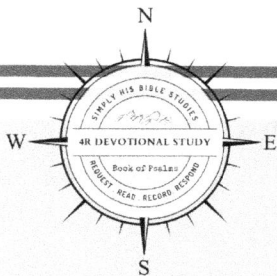

Psalm 74

Request: Lord, help me to read and then apply your teachings from this psalm today. Give me an alert and eager mind, ready to do Your will. In Jesus' Name, Amen.

Read: Psalm 74

Record: Write down one verse from this passage that stood out to you.

Respond: Write a short prayer, talking to God about that verse.

I was so puzzled when I read this psalm and realized Asaph, a contemporary of David, had written it. David had just made Jerusalem his capital city and, as far as I remembered the story, no one had burned it to ruins yet. How could this be? I was so thrilled to read the Bible reference to Asaph the "seer" in 2 Chronicles 29:30. Ahhh, I thought. Asaph saw ahead to the time of Jerusalem's destruction and composed a song about it, ready to be sung by those who would witness it.

Can you imagine the horror of those who suffered through and survived the razing of Jerusalem? It has happened more than once throughout Israel's history, and Asaph's psalm has been helpful time and again. I am so glad he captured the horror and misery of those who saw Jerusalem ruined, not receiving the miracles for which they most likely hoped and prayed.

It is okay to grieve when your own personal Jerusalem comes tumbling down. Whether it's a death of a loved one for whom you begged for a miracle, the death of a marriage, or some other great calamity, the first response is almost always a cry of rejection and pain. This psalm can provide the words for those who grieve. God sees our hurt and the ravages of our broken hearts. He knows we feel unloved when we beg and He does not heal. Let's speak the words out loud and direct them to Him. Once we do, He can begin the work of healing in our hearts. He cries with us for the brokenness of this world.

Asaph doesn't stay in this place of grief and agony, though. He moves on to remember Who God is, despite allowing Jerusalem to be destroyed. God can still part a sea if He chooses. God is able to crush huge, terrifying sea monsters. He made the seasons and the stars and the sun. He is that big. And so, even in the midst of destruction, Asaph asks again for the rescue of God's people.

We can, too. We can ask for help in recovery, in understanding, and in healing. We can keep turning to the God who is good even when our circumstances are not.

This kind of faith is deep. God is so pleased with us when we can go on believing in Him even in the hardest of times. There is comfort nowhere else. Let's always run to Him when our walls crumble and our hopes fade. Of this we can be sure: He knows, He cares, and He stands with us in the ruins. He is able to help us rebuild.

My verse: "Why do you hold back your strong right hand? Unleash your powerful fist and destroy them" (Psalm 74:11).

My response: Father, we often don't understand why You allow wickedness to flourish! I'm so thankful for honest questions in this psalm that remind me that I, your child, can also come to You and ask why.

Additional Study Options:

What did you learn about God from Psalm 74? Add to your list in the Study Notes section at the back of this book or in your own journal.

Read All the Psalms Plan: Read Psalms 75-76.

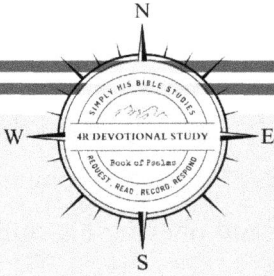

Psalm 78

Request: Father, help me to remember that rich or poor, I am always, always rich because I belong to You. You are the King of kings! Thank You for Your everlasting love, Your tenderness, Your watch-care over me. As I read today, come near and show me what You have for me today. In Jesus' Name, Amen.

Read: Psalm 78

Record: Write down one verse from this passage that stood out to you.

Respond: Write a short prayer, talking to God about that verse.

_____

_____

_____

_____

_____

_____

_____

_____

This is the longest psalm you'll be asked to read in one sitting. Asaph has a lot to say in this instructive psalm. He sets out his purpose in writing this psalm in verse 7: "So each generation should set its hope anew on God, not forgetting his glorious miracles and obeying his commands." There it is. Asaph knows we can quickly forget how big and good our God is! He doesn't want us to walk through rituals and become just cultural followers because that's what our parents did. Nope. He wants *each generation to set its hope anew.* What a wonderful prayer to pray for our children and grandchildren, nieces and nephews!

The entirety of this psalm is about this one central message. Stay close to God. Remember all He has done. Do not walk away from Him. Asaph teaches us lessons from Israel's troubled history. He lays out once again all the ways God has blessed and helped His people. He reminds us that despite these great blessings, they still whined and complained and got bored with God, choosing to follow their selfish desires that ended in destruction. So incredibly sad.

There are very relevant and good lessons for us in this passage. It is not enough to go through the motions. As Christians, we can check a lot of boxes that make us "look good" in the Christian community. If we attend church, serve on committees, give money to the poor, and are faithful in attending small groups, we can feel pretty much all set. Those great choices do make us more likely to be close to God. However, it is possible to do all those things with a cold heart. Asaph says it like this: "But all they gave him was lip service; they lied to him with their tongues. Their hearts were not loyal to him. They did not keep his covenant" (Psalm 78:36, 37).

How is your heart? Are you able to end a quiet time with a whispered, "Thy will be done in all things, Lord, in my life today?" I find the best way to test my heart is in praying a prayer like that. A surrendered prayer that wants His will above my own. When I struggle to pray that, I have

to look deep within. What am I afraid of? What do I cling to that I think might be better than His will? Do I trust that He is good and that surrendering to Him will yield the best results?

There was a time when I was consumed with fear praying for God's will above my own. The enemy of my soul whispered lies to me. If I prayed for God's will, God would smite me with cancer, allow my loved ones to die, and take away my home. Yup. What vicious lies. God is not waiting for our surrender so He can harm us. Let's remember Jesus' words of reassurance in Matthew: "You parents—if your children ask for a loaf of bread, do you give them a stone instead? Or if they ask for a fish, do you give them a snake? Of course not! So if you sinful people know how to give good gifts to your children, how much more will your heavenly Father give good gifts to those who ask him" (Matthew 7:9-11).

Give yourself to Him as a daily surrender. Confirm that you want Him to lead and you will follow. Keep your heart soft toward Him. Bad things will sometimes happen to you whether or not you pray for God's will to be done. But if you've prayed that prayer, the good times will be so much richer. Even the bad times will be better because He will be right there, welcomed by you into the troubles and able to help you bear them. Let's not forget the Lord or give Him only lip service. Let's give Him our hearts. Let's pray diligently that those in the next generation will walk with the One who alone can make the path straight and right and good and full of joy!

My verse: "So each generation should set its hope anew on God, not forgetting his glorious miracles and obeying his commands" (Psalm 78:7).

My response: Lord, help Ray and me to share the stories of Your faithfulness—and the consequences we suffered when we disobeyed—with our grandchildren. May they set their hope on You, Lord! And may they not forget all You did for Your people and for our family. May they obey Your commands and choose to follow You faithfully, sharing the heritage with their own grandchildren someday.

Additional Study Options:

What did you learn about God from Psalm 78? Add to your list in the Study Notes section at the back of this book or in your own journal.

Read All the Psalms Plan: Read Psalms 77.

Before Ray and I had children, I taught English and French to middle schoolers in a Christian school. I loved those kids! After getting a couple of years under my belt, teaching was a joy. I'd figured out how to keep the class under control, and I genuinely enjoyed my days. At some point, I must have told the students about my quiet times. They were not as consistent back then, but I did have them most mornings before I left to teach for the day. I told them that I was a nicer teacher because I stopped to meet with God first before I saw them.

Well. On one particular day, everything had gone wrong at home. I probably got up late, and perhaps Ray needed extra assistance. I don't remember the details, but I do know that I did not have a quiet time. I not only didn't meet with God. I didn't think about Him or even toss up a "help me" prayer. I came to school rather grumpy and unsettled. This was not good.

After enduring the crabby version of Mrs. Gamble, a rather brave and intrepid seventh grade boy raised his hand. "Yes?" I said in a clipped voice. "Mrs. Gamble," he said, "we are all just kind of wondering if you had your quiet time this morning?"

My mouth dropped open. There was a long moment of silence. I thought back. Had I had my quiet time? No, I had not. I repented in front of those precious, bewildered-by-my-anger young teens. I told them how far from being right with God I was that morning. We all agreed that I was much, much nicer when I met with God first!

Oh, this lesson has stuck with me over the years. When I am tempted to not open the Word and spend at least a few moments reading and praying, I remember how poorly I do without God leading me. Even five minutes with God can reset my mind and spirit so that I am yielded to Him, and He is able to use me for good and not harm. Don't skip time with God. Your family and friends will be so much better off if you've met with Him first and are walking under His guidance for the day!

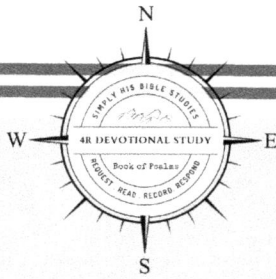

Psalm 81

Request: Father God, help me to treat all who cross my path today with Your love and kindness. I need You. Oh, I need You! Be near me as I open Your Word today. In Jesus' Name, Amen.

Read: Psalm 81

Record: Write down one verse from this passage that stood out to you.

Respond: Write a short prayer, talking to God about that verse.

This is the last psalm of Asaph that we are going to study. His psalm contributions end with Psalm 83. If you are choosing to read all the psalms, you will finish Asaph's psalms tomorrow. He begins this psalm urging the people of Israel to sing praises to God and lists all the instruments that should be used in their worship: tambourine, lyre, harp, and ram's horn. He wants this praise to be loud and full and robust! He reminds the people of Israel to come together at festival times and to blow the ram's horn at new and full moons. He's gearing everyone up to shout out songs of praise.

But then there is an abrupt change. Perhaps as Asaph was writing these words of instruction, God stepped in and changed the song being written. Because he was a prophet or seer, Asaph heard from God in a unique and vivid way. In verse five, Asaph hears a voice, and although he calls it an "unknown voice," we realize very quickly that the voice he heard was God's.

All of a sudden, the call to worship is halted. Instead, God speaks through Asaph to His people directly. I love that Asaph kept the first part of the psalm intact. It's almost like he was saying, "This was what I was going to write when God interrupted me. What God had to say was more important, so here it is." God is the speaker for the remainder of the psalm.

God warns His people to follow Him and no other gods. He tells them the good things He has waiting for them if they simply follow Him. He reminds them of the times He saved them in the past. "For it was I, the LORD your God, who rescued you from the land of Egypt. Open your mouth wide, and I will fill it with good things" (Psalm 81:10). You know what imagery comes to my mind when I read that verse? I see a little bird with its beak stretched as wide as it can go, being lovingly fed by its parents. God often tells us that He covers us with His wings. He also longs to fill us full if we would stop and open our mouths to receive all His goodness!

One of the saddest verses in this psalm comes a bit later. "Oh, that my people would listen to me! Oh, that Israel would follow me, walking in my paths!" (Psalm 81:13). God can do anything. However, He will not interfere with our ability to make choices. To force the Israelites to walk that good path would require God to take away their free will. They would be slaves all over again. He wanted the Israelites, and He wants us, to follow Him willingly and joyfully out of trust and love. This is what blesses our great God's heart! And when we do choose to follow Him, we are satisfied as ". . . with wild honey from the rock" (Psalm 81:16b).

My verse: "But I would feed you with the finest wheat. I would satisfy you with wild honey from the rock" (Psalm 81:16).

My response: If we would but listen and obey, we would see such blessings. Father, when I am tested, help me to wait in patient trust, knowing You ultimately have good and not harm in store for me. Forgive me when I reject the finest fare and instead settle for stale bread and sour milk.

Additional Study Options:

What did you learn about God from Psalm 81? Add to your list in the Study Notes section at the back of this book or in your own journal.

Read All the Psalms Plan: Read Psalms 79, 82.

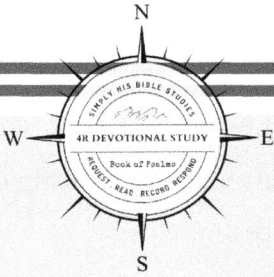

Psalm 84

Request: Thank You, Lord, for my brothers and sisters around the world who are also stopping to read Your Word today. We are all Your people, the sheep of Your pasture. I join them in longing for a word from You! Teach me, Lord. In Jesus' Name, Amen.

Read: Psalm 84

Record: Write down one verse from this passage that stood out to you.

Respond: Write a short prayer, talking to God about that verse.

What a beautiful psalm we were able to study today! The descendants (or sons) of Korah, who worked in the temple, created for us a psalm of longing and joy. It points us to the worship of God as a community. I'd like to focus on some repeated thoughts in the psalm.

First, a strong thread of joy runs through these verses. A deep, welling-up-inside gladness that goes beyond a surface feeling. There's joy as we dwell in God's presence, not just in a temple or tabernacle, but because His Spirit dwells in our hearts (vs. 4). We feel joy when His strength enables us to move toward Him (vs. 5). We experience great joy when we trust in God (vs. 12)! Following God is not drudgery and misery. He takes away our shame and clothes us in righteousness because of His Son's death on our behalf. He frees us from our burdens. He delights in us. He holds us closely. He takes away our fears. We can experience joy even in the midst of sorrow as we remember whose we are and the beautiful inheritance awaiting us in Heaven.

Second, God is addressed as the LORD of Heaven's Armies three times. Think about that title for God. Have you ever seen an angel? I haven't. I can remember a time when I was a young wife, alone in our home, when Ray was away on a military deployment. There were strange noises in the house—creaks and squeaks that made me jump. I prayed and asked God to send angels to guard me. I started picturing them in my mind's eye standing by my bed. The thought of those huge, other worldly beings both comforted and terrified me. (I prayed that God would keep them invisible, coward that I am!)

Often, when a person in the Bible sees an angel, they're terrified! They fall down as though dead. They have to be reassured to not be afraid. These beings are big! And yet, when we pray to the LORD of Heaven's Armies, we are praying to the One who is even bigger and grander. He's the

One these mighty beings obey. This is the God we serve. The One who commands heavenly beings! That itself brings a rush of joy and WOW to me!

I sort of "danced" my way through this psalm as I read it, knowing we have the privilege of being in God's presence every moment because the Holy Spirit lives in us. I'm so thankful that I share that joy with you and millions of other Christians around the globe. All of us worshiping the one true God! Church fellowship is such a joy, as well, when we come together and lift our voices in unity to praise Him! Today, let's celebrate that being a Christian means being joy-filled with hope and longing, knowing that we are loved and held.

My verse: "O LORD of Heaven's Armies, what joy for those who trust in you" (Psalm 84:12).

My response: The joy is not in circumstances. It's in You—The Mighty One—who commands angels and heavenly beings who would frighten me if I were to see them. You, LORD God, bring rich joy to those who are Your very own. I rejoice in that today!

Additional Study Options:

What did you learn about God from Psalm 84? Add to your list in the Study Notes section at the back of this book or in your own journal.

Read All the Psalms Plan: Read Psalms 83, 85.

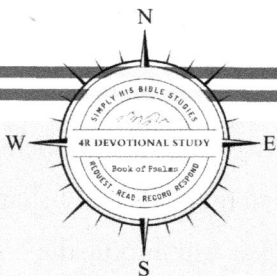

Psalm 86

Request: Bend down, O LORD, and hear my prayer; answer me, for I need your help . . . Teach me your ways, O LORD, that I may live according to your truth! (Psalm 86:1,11a). In Jesus' Name, Amen.

Read: Psalm 86

Record: Write down one verse from this passage that stood out to you.

Respond: Write a short prayer, talking to God about that verse.

How is your time alone with God going? Are you finding a rhythm in going to God first to study His Word, and then reading my thoughts? I hope so. My goal is for you and God to meet first. That is the most important. My words are a supplement to the main course—His Word!

This psalm is a beautiful prayer from start to finish. If you can't find the words when you feel attacked by others, turn to Psalm 86 and pray it from your heart to the Lord! We read of David's concern midway through the psalm: "O God, insolent people rise against me; a violent gang is trying to kill me. You mean nothing to them" (Psalm 86:14). David is being chased by those who have no fear of God. There's no use in reasoning with them that God would want them to be kind. They don't have ears to hear it. Despite his distress, most of this psalm is focused on David's need for God and his worship of God. David does not dwell on his troubles. We should follow his example. Dwelling on our problems takes over our minds in an unhealthy way, causing fear and anxiety to grow. Instead, like David, let's turn to the Lord, tell Him our difficulties and then remember who He is and how He can help us.

Notice David's humility as he begins this psalm. He needs help. He asks for it. He asks God to "bend down," reflecting a proper understanding of Who God is (big) and who David is (small). David comes in confidence, knowing that God, his Shepherd, will bend down and help his little struggling sheep.

As David asks for help, he intersperses beautiful verses that remind him (and us) of the astounding character of God. God is good, ready to forgive, and full of unfailing love for those who ask for help. God answers us when we call to Him. God performs wonderful deeds. He grants purity of heart and teaches us His ways. He is able to rescue us from death. God is compassionate and merciful, slow to get angry. He is faithful. He gives us strength. He helps and comforts us. Wow.

I can't think of a better way to feel comforted than to dwell on God's character. To remember that no matter who is against us, if we have received Jesus as Savior and Lord, we always have God with us. God is so very, very good. Rejoice in that today and remind yourself often that you do not walk alone. He is with you. You are held.

My verse: "Be merciful to me, O Lord, for I am calling on you constantly" (Psalm 86:3).

My response: I am struck by how David called to You constantly, Lord. Help me to be like him, never ceasing to abide in You, intentionally and intimately sharing every moment with You.

Additional Study Options:

What did you learn about God from Psalm 86? Add to your list in the Study Notes section at the back of this book or in your own journal.

Read All the Psalms Plan: Read Psalm 87.

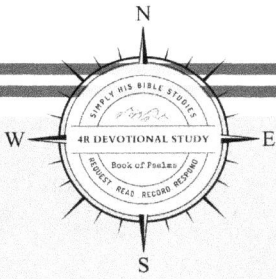

N
W   E
S

SIMPLY HIS BIBLE STUDIES
4R DEVOTIONAL STUDY
Book of Psalms
REQUEST · READ · RECORD · RESPOND

Psalm 88

Request: Thank You, Lord, that You are always with me. Right now, as I open Your Word, You are here. Help me to be aware of Your presence and approach the reading with a deep desire to learn from You. In Jesus' Name, Amen.

Read: Psalm 88

Record: Write down one verse from this passage that stood out to you.

Respond: Write a short prayer, talking to God about that verse.

Psalm 88 might be the darkest psalm in the whole Book of Psalms. And I love that it's in the Bible. Have you ever experienced a time in your life of deep depression? I have, just once. I remember the heaviness and hopelessness of that time. Everything I did took supreme effort. Folding one basket of laundry felt insurmountable. Smiling back at someone in church? Impossible. My darkness lasted about three months. Some people suffer much, much longer. Yet coming out of that season took time and effort. I would list one or two things on my fridge that were to be accomplished in the day. Simple things. Get dressed. Wash dishes. Slowly, as I succeeded at those, I added more. I prayed. Ray prayed. In God's mercy, the heavy cloak of darkness lifted. I am so thankful for that awful time. It's given me a greater empathy for those who suffer from depression.

This psalm does not try to make depression look superficial or easily fixed, does it? But what it does do is quite profound. Despite the lack of answers, despite the feeling that God caused all this or, at the very least, allowed it . . . despite all that . . . we still pray. We still seek Him. We still go to Him with our grief. We name our sorrows before Him and keep coming and keep coming and keep coming. We have faith in a God who "seems" to have turned a deaf ear to us. We believe anyway.

Eventually, the darkness will lift. Joy will come. And by staying close to the God who never leaves us, even in the pit of despair, we are not lost. We still have Him. Right there. Holding us whether we can feel it or not. It is so good to know that depression is not new or unique to us. There are times when, as the psalmist writes, it feels like only darkness is left. And yet? The psalmist prays because God is still there, and darkness is not dark to Him.

There was a time in Jesus' life when many followers deserted Him. John tells us about it in John 6. Jesus

said some things that were hard to understand, causing people to walk away instead of drawing near to learn more. Jesus looked at His twelve disciples and asked if they, too, were going to leave Him. Here's the answer Peter gave: "Simon Peter replied, 'Lord, to whom would we go? You have the words that give eternal life. We believe, and we know you are the Holy One of God'" (John 6:68-69).

To leave God in a time of darkness is so foolish. No. We hold on all the tighter to Him. He is in the darkness with us. We pray day after weary day. Our faith is a gift to Him who loves us and has allowed this hard thing. And one day, perhaps when we least expect it, we will find ourselves smiling and even laughing again! Oh, the joy that follows that sorrow is very great indeed!

My verse: "O LORD, I cry out to you. I will keep pleading day by day" (Psalm 88:13).

My response: Oh, Father! The sadness in this psalm seems to be without relief. Yet Heman the Ezrahite, a descendant of Korah, continues to cry out to You, cling to You, and ask for relief. His faith amazes me. His example challenges me. Help me to be as faith-filled if terrible days of pain come to me.

Additional Study Options:

What did you learn about God from Psalm 88? Add to your list in the Study Notes section at the back of this book or in your own journal.

Read All the Psalms Plan: Read Psalm 89.

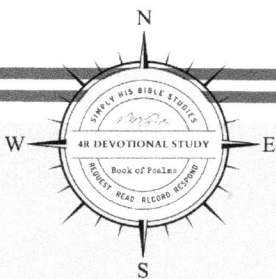

Psalm 91

Request: Dear Father, thank You for this little moment of time when the world around me fades, and You and I meet. Teach me, Lord. I am listening as I read. In Jesus' Name, Amen.

Read: Psalm 91

Record: Write down one verse from this passage that stood out to you.

Respond: Write a short prayer, talking to God about that verse.

Psalm 91 begins Book Four of the Psalms. This passage has comforted and quieted many a frantic soul. Soldiers in war zones read it. Weary caregivers cling to it. Those in trouble run to it. To me, reading Psalm 91 is like running, as a fearful child, to a parent who loves me. I imagine myself standing there afraid, and God, my perfect Parent, picks me up, holds me close, and rocks me. "Shhhhh," He whispers. "Don't fret. All will be well. You are safe with Me."

Let's notice a few key themes in this psalm. The first one is the **position** of the one in need. When in need, we should draw close to God. We find rest in the shadow of the Almighty. To be within His shadow is to be right next to Him. We come under His wings like a little bird nestled in a parent bird's underfeathers. This allows the weather-resistant overfeathers to keep the little one dry and protected from the storms raging around it. When in trouble, our position should be as close to God as possible.

Next, let's notice the **promises**. Because of eternal life, every promise we read in Psalm 91 will be true for every believer, either in this life or the heavenly life that follows. Ultimately, nothing will hurt us for long because we will be brought through to a place of safety. "If you make the LORD your refuge, if you make the Most High your shelter, no evil will conquer you . . ." declares the psalmist. (Psalm 91:9,10a) You might be buffeted, tried, and tested, but in the end, you will come into a beautiful place where evil is not allowed.

Last, let's talk about God's **protection**. Too often, when I am in trouble, I forget that God is with me and within me. Instead, I frantically try to solve the problem in my own strength. This doesn't work well for me. I try to control a chaotic situation and simply make it worse. I end up speaking words I regret, moving too fast, and making messes as I go. I am the kind of person I don't want to be. Me without God? Not pretty. When I remember that God is always with me and able to steady me throughout the circumstances, I can cope. When I remember He's near and cling to His big hand, the trials feel smaller and less overwhelming. I remember that *He's got me.* He is able to protect me. And if He allows something dreadful, He won't leave me to face it alone. He will not only walk into it with me, He will bring something good out of it that will blow my mind. He's that amazing.

My verse: "Those who live in the shelter of the Most High will find rest in the shadow of the Almighty" (Psalm 91:1).

My response: Oh, Father God! This verse calls me to stay close. You are my place of rest. Help me to abide in You and stay close to You all the days of my life. No storm will be able to overcome me because You are with me.

Additional Study Options:

What did you learn about God from Psalm 91? Add to your list in the Study Notes section at the back of this book or in your own journal.

Read All the Psalms Plan: Read Psalm 90.

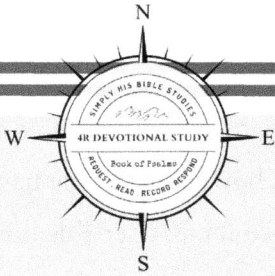

Psalm 92

Request: Keep me near You, Lord, my Shelter and Protector. Help me to nestle close today as I open Your Word. Please show me what I need to know for the day ahead. In Jesus' Name, Amen.

Read: Psalm 92

Record: Write down one verse from this passage that stood out to you.

Respond: Write a short prayer, talking to God about that verse.

_____

_____

_____

_____

_____

_____

_____

What a happy psalm! How lovely that it was created to be sung on the Sabbath. God tells us to rest one day out of seven in order to bring us delight. It's so sad to think how often people have taken a good thing (to rest and focus on the One who made us) and turned it into a terrible burden (rules, rules, rules on how to do it exactly "right").

Back when my daughters were in high school, I finally decided I should take this sabbath command to heart. Before then, I had believed nine of the Ten Commandments applied to my life, but the one about the sabbath was optional. God called me to study the sabbath. I learned so much about how God intended it to be and how often it is perverted into something dreadful.

This is where I landed. I believe that God wired our human bodies to need "extra rest" one day a week. We can work hard for many days in a row, but if we don't stop, we will break. I was in danger of breaking when I realized I needed to stop. So, I now get my chores done approximately before sundown on a Saturday night, and then I rest until approximately sundown on Sunday night. It's lovely. We attend church. I take long walks. I read books and nap. And with glee and full permission from God, I refuse to do my normal chores! Jesus tells us God made the sabbath for man. (Mark 2:27). He knew we would need rest.

He wants us to delight in His beautiful world, spend time in worship, and take pleasure in the change of pace that sabbath brings. It's fun!! (I do believe God is pleased when a pastor, nurse, or others—who often work on Sundays by necessity—choose an alternate sabbath day in which to rest and spend time with Him. Fires happen on Sundays, and I am awfully glad Christian firemen still come out to stop the flames. But even a fireman needs a day of rest . . . even if it has to be an alternate day.) Do your own searching. Ask God to show you His plan for you in keeping the sabbath.

In Psalm 92, our psalmist delights in the sabbath day. He gives us some great ways to praise God for His faithfulness and unfailing love. He calls on us to bring instruments and play a song for Him. He marvels at creation and the great works of God. He delights in God's love for His people even when they are old. He declares that those who belong to Him remain "vital and green," still praising God in their last days as they anticipate someday receiving new, beautiful bodies in Heaven! Let's declare with the psalmist every day, "The LORD is just! He is my rock! There is no evil in him!" (Psalm 92:15). Amen.

My verse: "But the godly will flourish like palm trees and grow strong like the cedars of Lebanon. For they are transplanted to the LORD's own house. They flourish in the courts of our God" (Psalm 92:12-13).

My response: How I thank You that You chose me, this Gentile girl, and adopted me into Your family. Transplanted. Reborn. Your daughter with access to You! Help me, Lord, to flourish and grow strong even in my old age.

Additional Study Options:

What did you learn about God from Psalm 92? Add to your list in the Study Notes section at the back of this book or in your own journal.

Read All the Psalms Plan: Read Psalms 93-94.

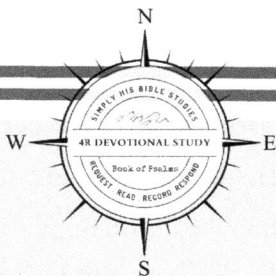

Psalm 95

Request: Teach me, Lord. In Jesus' Name and for His glory. Amen.

Read: Psalm 95

Record: Write down one verse from this passage that stood out to you.

Respond: Write a short prayer, talking to God about that verse.

We find a great reminder to be thankful in Psalm 95. Oh, how we need reminding! This psalm encourages us to be grateful and to notice all God has done. The psalmist gives us the reason for gratitude toward the end of the psalm. Let's start there.

God's patience was sorely tried when the people of Israel were in the wilderness. They had been slaves for hundreds of years, and there were thousands of them at this point. Some Bible scholars believe there may have been over a million of them. The Got Questions website estimates 30,000 to two million people. (https://www.gotquestions.org/Israelites-exodus.html). Whatever the number, there were a LOT of them. They'd cried out to God to save them, and He had—quite miraculously. He sent all sorts of plagues and torments upon the Egyptians until finally Pharoah let the Israelites go free and leave his country. Their Egyptian captors could not wait to get them out due to the plagues that had beset them, so they even sent them away with gifts! When Pharoah changed his mind and went after them, God made the sea waters separate, creating a dry path for this huge nation to walk through without even getting their toes wet. Then . . . God swallowed up the army behind them.

So. The people of Israel had seen incredible miracles. Over and over God had proved Himself to them. He had led them through the wilderness with a pillar of fire. He had rained food (manna) down on them day after day. They had lived in a world of miraculous intervention and care. Astounding. Mind-boggling. Imagine God's sadness in Meribah when they complained because they had no water to quench their thirst. Instead of trusting, they got angry, belligerent and downright mean. What ought to have been their response? What would have happened if they had stopped where God had brought them and asked for His help, fully expecting He would provide? Wouldn't that have been beautiful? How soon we forget what God has done. Let's be careful. We, too, can be like the Israelites at Meribah (and again later in Massah) and complain instead of pray and trust.

Now let's go back to the beginning of this psalm. A quick read-through of Psalm 95 led me to this list of gifts from God for which we all should continually be grateful!

- God is our Rock on whom we can depend.
- God saved us. He literally is our salvation.
- God is King of all, and we belong to Him!
- God holds the depths of the earth and the mountains in His hands. They're not caving in on us.
- God chose to make us and give us life.
- God watches over us, His people.
- We are under His care.

I could add so many more things. I am an American living in incredible comfort. I have hot water at the turn of a tap. I have a roof over my head. I have more than enough clothing to wear and food to eat. I have legs that work. I can breathe without struggle. I am able to admire little birds and trees right outside my window. I have access to a Bible, the precious living Word of God. Let's not allow present troubles to cause us to forget the forever-blessings given to us by the living, loving God!

My verse: "For the LORD is a great God, a great King above all gods" (Psalm 95:3).

My response: You are great, LORD God. There is no one like You—no god except You—King of kings, supreme over all. I am so very thankful that I am Yours.

Additional Study Options:

What did you learn about God from Psalm 95? Add to your list in the Study Notes section at the back of this book or in your own journal.

Read All the Psalms Plan: Read Psalms 96-97.

Just three weeks left in our walk through the Psalms, God's songbook! Have you discovered more and more about God's amazing character? I hope so. I hope you've also come to appreciate the freedom God gives us to approach Him in any mood or situation, laying our hearts out before Him, knowing He genuinely wants to hear from us. Are you interested in going deeper? Let me share something with you that has blessed me immensely over the last couple of decades of my life. I call it a Selah Day.

This practice is truly a "little touch of Heaven" each month! I boldly mark out a day on my calendar and write Selah Day on it. Even though the actual time spent with God is only 4-6 hours, I like keeping the whole day free on my calendar. I can then take that time to just "be" with the Lord.

How I spend the day varies by season, budget, and emotional needs. I keep a Selah Day bag at the ready for these days. In it is a Bible with lots of study notes and word definitions from the original Hebrew and Greek. I only use it on a Selah Day, and it's fantastic for following rabbit trails when I have the time to do that. I have a pen case with pens, a journal, and several good Christian books that only get read on that special day. The bag goes with me, and sometimes I spend a lot of time reading, writing, and studying, and sometimes I don't. I try to yield to what the Spirit tells me to do. I might drive to the ocean and take a long, leisurely walk admiring the ocean and the clouds in the sky. I might sit in my car and pray, watching the waves. I might go to a coffee shop where no one knows me and journal. Sometimes, I stay home and sit out on my deck (warm weather) or light a fire (cold weather), shut my office door tight, and invest in quieting my soul and praying, reading, napping, and loving the Lord.

Do you know what happens when I give this time over to the Lord? Peace. The world continues to spin without me. The chores all wait for me. After I settle in to the quiet, I enter a place of what the Bible calls *shalom*. Whether you have two hours or six, I highly recommend the Selah Day. Give it a try. It is always a blessing.

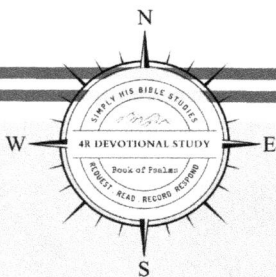

Psalm 99-100

Request: "Speak, Lord, in the stillness, while I wait on Thee; hush my heart to listen, in expectancy." In Jesus' Name, Amen. (from the hymn by Emily Crawford, *Speak, Lord, in the Stillness*)

Read: Psalms 99-100

Record: Write down one verse from this passage that stood out to you.

Respond: Write a short prayer, talking to God about that verse.

What a lovely pair psalms 99 and 100 make. Psalm 99 is full of praise for our mighty, holy God, and Psalm 100 follows with a song of thanksgiving, delighting that He is ours and we are His. How amazing is that?

Psalm 99 calls God holy. Let's talk about that word for a moment. The Hebrew word is *qadosh* or *kadesh*. Definitions include: set apart for a specific purpose, consecrated, sacred, pure, morally blameless. God is the holy One, the only One who is not created, who always was and always will be. He is sooooo different from us. There's a purity about Him, and a "not like us" quality to Him that is unique and awesome beyond words. When we call God holy, we give Him high praise for His unique and powerful and beautiful Being.

Psalm 99 opens with the response we should have when we think about God and His holiness: "The Lord is king! Let the nations tremble! He sits on his throne between the cherubim. Let the whole earth quake!" (Psalm 99:1). Notice all the exclamation marks just in verse 1. The Lord is . . . Wow. Beyond our ability to truly fathom. This "otherness" of God leads nations to tremble and the entire earth to quake. He is that big, that powerful, that awe-inspiring. This is a great psalm to pray or sing in worship.

Psalm 100 calls us to worship Him and be grateful for Him. Not only is God high and mighty and holy, He is also our Shepherd, and we are His sheep. We are able to have a close and loving relationship with God because of His great, condescending love for us. He wants us. It's unfathomable. We are under His care. It's remarkable. Oh, how grateful we should be that this immense God chooses to walk with us! Yes, we should tremble and quake, but Psalm 100 reminds us that if we've come to Him in faith and are His, being in His presence should make us happy.

"Shout with joy to the LORD, all the earth! Worship the LORD with gladness. Come before him, singing with joy" (Psalm 100:1-2). God inspires awe. Because He stoops down to love us, He inspires gladness. Be glad, friend! You are loved by the King of kings, the holy One. Wow, indeed.

My verse: "Worship the LORD with gladness. Come before him, singing with joy" (Psalm 100:2).

My response: Lord, we exalt You. We are in awe of You. Because of Your unfathomable love for us, we can come into Your presence with joy! You make our hearts glad.

Additional Study Options:

What did you learn about God from Psalms 99-100? Add to your list in the Study Notes section at the back of this book or in your own journal.

Read All the Psalms Plan: Read Psalm 98.

Psalm 103

Request: Dear Shepherd of my soul, please feed me as I read from Your Word today and show me how to live for You. In Jesus' Name, Amen.

Read: Psalm 103

Record: Write down one verse from this passage that stood out to you.

Respond: Write a short prayer, talking to God about that verse.

_____

_____

_____

_____

_____

_____

_____

_____

Sometimes it's hard to remember all the good things we have and all the times God has blessed us. When I am feeling sick, and my whole body aches, it's not easy to remember healthy times when all was well. When I've lost a loved one or struggled through the valley with a close friend, my mind does not naturally turn to thoughts of thanksgiving for God's goodness. I can get stuck in a deep and gloomy fog quite easily.

As we've talked about earlier, sometimes there is a need to lament and be sad. Not every day is a happy day. In fact, God warns us over and over again that many of our days here on earth will be hard. We're told to "take up our cross" and patiently endure difficult circumstances. We are warned that we might be persecuted and reviled because we are followers of Jesus. It's not always pretty here on earth, and the psalms have taught us to bring our sorrows to the Lord.

However, there's a point when lament turns to bitterness, self-pity, depression, and even anger. The enemy turns a legitimate cry for help and rescue into turning away from the only One who can truly help us. May God show us when we need to turn to a psalm like Psalm 103 and remember the goodness of God in the midst of the pain. No matter how bad it gets, God is still good. Still there. Still enabling us to move and live and breathe and see the beauty of a night sky. If I can't come up with reasons to be thankful, I can turn to Psalm 103 and read it out loud to my soul. This revives a weary heart in ways beyond what I can describe. Thanksgiving can truly be a weapon against the enemies of discouragement and anxiety.

I've developed the practice of recording in a journal those special times when God has met a need or comforted my heart. It's my own little book of songs to Him. This is a treasure trove of sweet memories where I've recalled all God has done and cheered myself up, knowing He hasn't changed and He is able to act again—often in ways beyond what I could ask or imagine. If you are a writer, I recommend this! Let's be a thankful people. Let's not allow hardship to cloud our minds and pull us away from the truth. God does love and care for His people, even when He allows hard things to happen.

My verse: "He fills my life with good things. My youth is renewed like the eagle's!" (Psalm 103:5).

My response: Lord, You do fill my life with good things—so many of which I take for granted. Plenty of food, fresh, unpolluted hot and cold water, clothing, shelter, good friends, and a dear family. Help me to see the good, even on days that are hard. And thank You that I can still feel young, renewed like the eagles soaring high above, even as I get older. Only You, dear Father, can do this—and You do!

Additional Study Options:

What did you learn about God from Psalm 103? Add to your list in the Study Notes section at the back of this book or in your own journal.

Read All the Psalms Plan: Read Psalms 101-102.

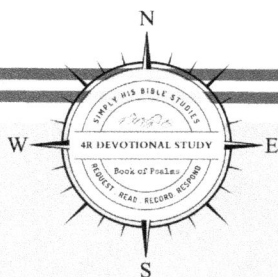

Psalm 104

Request: Thank You, Father, for another day of life. Use me today for Your good purposes and teach me as I stop to read Your Word. In Jesus' Name, Amen.

Read: Psalm 104

Record: Write down one verse from this passage that stood out to you.

Respond: Write a short prayer, talking to God about that verse.

It was a typical busy day at my house. I'd risen early and made my husband his lunch, set out his breakfast, and ironed his clothes. I'd sat and done my quiet time, quickly dressed and walked the dog. I returned to do laundry, make a grocery list, fold last week's clean laundry still in the baskets, and then I headed to my home office to work. By mid-morning, I felt completely done. And yet, there was much more to do, and it was only 10:30 AM. Ever felt that way? You push and strive and check off items on the list, and all of a sudden, the energy leaves and you're toast. That was me.

Furthermore, the sun was shining through my office window and the azure blue sky was calling to me. Well then. Time for a mid-morning break for sure. I made myself a cup of tea, grabbed a blanket for my legs as it was still a bit chilly despite the sun, and plunked myself down on a chair on our little deck. And there I sat. Doing absolutely nothing.

After a few minutes, I started to notice things. The leaves had just begun reappearing on the trees with that fresh, shiny, light green of early spring. As I watched the leaves move softly in a light breeze, I heard a bird song. So pretty! I watched two squirrels chase each other from one tree branch to another so rapidly that I thought they'd lose their grip and tumble to the ground. They did not. They were just having fun on this glorious spring morning. Clouds drifted by, and my heart rate slowed. Ahhhh.

This. This is what I needed. A half-hour in God's beautiful, calm, unhurried creation to soothe my soul and slow me down. I smiled, lifting my tea cup in a toast to the Creator who made all this for me! I shook my head at my own foolishness. This beauty was right outside my door, and I almost missed it. Being outside that morning not only restored my soul, it renewed my energy. When I went back to the office and my desk, it was with a lighter step and a new joy.

Our psalm today brings us deep into the world of creation. It's best to read it slowly with the imagination fully activated. If you have the time to read it twice this morning, read it out loud.

Marvel with the psalmist at all the wonders of this complex, amazing world made by the God of the universe. And remember to go outside and actually be in it. Man can make some pretty amazing things, but nothing is as beautiful as God's creation. Savor it, and compliment Him on it. It's a sure mood-lifter!

My verse: "You are dressed in a robe of light. You stretch out the starry curtain of the heavens" (Psalm 104:2).

My response: Unfathomable, mighty God, I loved reading these poetic descriptions of You. My God and my King, there is none like You. Thank You for songs like this one that remind me of Your incredible creative power, bringing such beauty to us who dwell on the earth!

Additional Study Options:

What did you learn about God from Psalm 104? Add to your list in the Study Notes section at the back of this book or in your own journal.

Read All the Psalms Plan: Read Psalms 105-106.

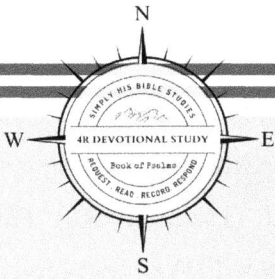

Psalm 107

Request: Help me to live this day well, Lord, as I come to You for help by opening Your Word. In Jesus' Name, Amen.

Read: Psalm 107

Record: Write down one verse from this passage that stood out to you.

Respond: Write a short prayer, talking to God about that verse.

_____

_____

_____

_____

_____

     _____

     _____

     _____

     _____

What an incredible psalm this is! Psalm 107 begins Book Five of the Book of Psalms. We learn why the author wrote it waaaay down at the end in the final verse: "Those who are wise will take all this to heart; they will see in our history the faithful love of the Lord" (Psalm 107:43). This psalm will enable us to take heart when troubles come our way. And they will. When we look at our lives as a whole, we will see God's faithfulness and help throughout. It's a lovely psalm and so specific to the various troubles that can come our way. Let's look at each category together.

Extreme Poverty. The homeless can be found across our planet and probably in each of our hometowns. They have no place to lay their weary heads. They don't know where they will get their next meal. I can't imagine that kind of desperation. The psalmist assures us that even in those dire straits, God is able to rescue. (Psalm 107:4-9)

Imprisonment. There are different kinds of prisons. We can be confined in jail, locked up because of something terrible we have done, or because of false accusations. We can be in an emotional or mental prison, trapped by continual memories of the past that rob us of our sleep. The psalmist assures us that even in these terrifying situations, God is able to rescue. (Psalm 107:10-16)

Foolishness. We can be our own worst enemy. We can worry so much about weight gain that we don't eat enough of the food God provides for our enjoyment. We can eat too much of that good food. Oh, we can sometimes be quite foolish, not eating wisely or caring for ourselves appropriately. At times, we can't help it, but the people in this particular section could have behaved differently and didn't. Guess what? God rescues them, as well, when they cry out to Him. We don't have to be sensible and do all the right things to be rescued. Thank You, Lord! (Psalm 107:17-22)

Natural Disasters. Hurricanes. Tsunamis. Sink Holes. Blizzards. Tornadoes. Ocean Storms. Floods. Drought. Earthquakes. Mud Slides. The list goes on and on. We can be going about life and doing all the right things and, still, a wildfire can sweep through our neighborhood and destroy our home and all our possessions. Some troubles come to us for no apparent reason. Even then, God is able to rescue us from the situation or in the midst of it with His own special kind of peace and care. (Psalm 107:23-32)

No matter what, this psalm tells us, God will help us through whatever trials come into our lives. We can trust Him when life is easy, and we can trust Him when life is hard. We can cry out to Him in the midst of it all, and He will help us. Hallelujah! If you want further reassurance, I recommend reading Romans 8:31-39. Old Testament or New Testament, your God wants you to know He's with you always, in every situation.

My verse: "Those who are wise will take all this to heart; they will see in our history the faithful love of the Lord" (Psalm 107:43).

My response: Father, help me never forget my own moments of deliverance. Remembering the times You have rescued and strengthened me is a beautiful way to celebrate Your goodness.

Additional Study Options:

What did you learn about God from Psalm 107? Add to your list in the Study Notes section at the back of this book or in your own journal.

Read All the Psalms Plan: Read Psalms 108-109.

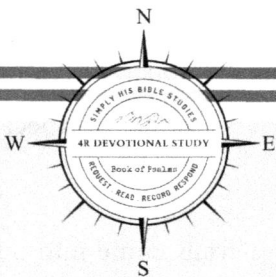

Psalm 111

Request: Help me, Lord, never to tire of meeting You in my daily quiet time. Help me to always seek You for the strength I need for each moment. Remind me that always, always, You love me. I'm so grateful. In Jesus' Name, Amen.

Read: Psalm 111

Record: Write down one verse from the passage that stood out to you.

Respond: Write a short prayer, talking to God about that verse.

Today, as I read through our psalm, I was struck by the very first verse: "Praise the LORD! I will thank the LORD with all my heart as I meet with his godly people" (Psalm 111:1). This is clearly a song to be sung with others in worship! I've just come through a challenging time in worship. In May 2023, I suddenly lost all the hearing in my left ear. It's an occurrence called *sudden sensorineural hearing loss*. I was familiar with it because years ago the same thing happened in my right ear. It was not caught soon enough, and I have such poor hearing in the right ear that I can't even utilize a hearing aid. There's not enough sound being received to amplify it.

When I became deaf, temporarily, in my left ear, my world was nearly silent. Thankfully, prednisone shots allowed my hearing to be restored to 70%-word recognition. I am now the happy owner of a hearing aid for that ear. However, with that second loss came an irreversible (outside of a miracle) loss of my ability to discern musical notes. I can't sing on tune, and I can't recognize most tunes anymore. This makes worship at church very, very strange.

When it first happened, I cried a lot. I missed singing, and the unpleasant sounds that emanated from those singing around me were frightening. I knew the music sounded beautiful to others, but it was dreadful for me. However, I believe that meeting together to worship and praise is a good and necessary thing for us to do (if we possibly can) as Christ-followers. So, I kept worshipping. Gradually, I learned to "chant" the words to the praise songs and hymns instead of singing them. I learned to rejoice that I am standing with others who love God, declaring to the best of my hearing-impaired ability truths about Him as we join our voices. It's beautiful again because we are standing in unity praising the one true God all together.

The psalms we've been reading for the past seven weeks declare wonderful truths about our God. Yes, they're truths we already know, but they're worth repeating over and over again. I don't know about you, but I personally love to be told "I love you" every day by my husband even though I have heard it for over 40 years. In the same way, we declare truths about God and tell Him how much we praise, love, and honor Him over and over. Once is not enough to say the things that matter most! As you choose a verse, don't feel that you have to respond with a brand-new thought. Choose a truth you know and love, and write it down. Marvel at the great God we serve and know that He never tires of hearing us tell Him of our love for Him!

My verse: "Fear of the LORD is the foundation of true wisdom. All who obey his commandments will grow in wisdom. Praise him forever!" (Psalm 111:10)

My response: I love that obedience to Your commands grows my wisdom. When I obey and see the results, I see all the more how wise and good You are—how Your commands are for our good and not harm.

Additional Study Options:

What did you learn about God from Psalm 111? Add to your list in the Study Notes section at the back of this book or in your own journal.

Read All the Psalms Plan: Read Psalm 110.

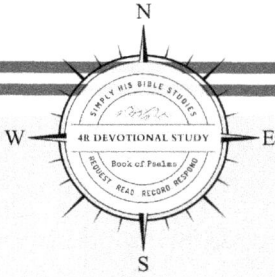

Psalm 112

Request: I love You, Lord! Help me to say it over and over and over again, delighting in the fact that You actually love me, too. Even on my worst days. Thank You for that forever kind of love! In Jesus' Name, Amen.

Read: Psalm 112

Record: Write down one verse from this passage that stood out to you.

Respond: Write a short prayer, talking to God about that verse.

_____

_____

_____

_____

_____

_____

_____

Let's start at the end of this psalm and then explore it as a whole. The last verse reads: "The wicked will see this and be infuriated. They will grind their teeth in anger; they will slink away, their hopes thwarted" (Psalm 112:10). Oh, what a picture this conjures up in my mind. Angry, wicked men slinking away, depressed at being unable to trip up or best the good guys. Whether we realize it or not, we all serve someone—either the Lord Almighty or His enemy, the devil. The wicked are enslaved to sin and the devil. Evidently, these wicked ones are decidedly evil and actively work against those who love the Lord. Well. Why are they so frustrated with the servants of the LORD? Let's go back and list some of the reasons from the psalm.

- Those who fear the LORD are first loyal to Him, obeying His commandments, and refusing to be enticed to join the bad guys.

- While godly parents may not have godly children (God was a great parent, yet many in Israel walked away!), it is more likely that children raised to know and love God will walk with Him as adults. This certainly angers the devil. Another generation lost to him and safely in God's Kingdom!

- Those who fear the LORD are generous with their wealth, giving to those in need and shining God's light into dark places with their servant hearts. This disrupts the devil's work.

- Those who fear God are not overcome by evil but plant their feet in the truth.

- They aren't afraid of bad news. The devil and his followers can't scare them. "...[T]hey confidently trust the LORD to care for them" (Psalm 112:7b).

What a joy to be reminded of the good that comes from following the Lord and obeying Him! We not only please Him, but we also thwart the enemy's plans and bring people into the light. So, don't be afraid! Walk boldly with the Lord, choosing the right, even when it's hard.

The bad guys who are enslaved by the devil will slink away. Or, maybe, just maybe, they will discover the light for themselves.

My verse: "Praise the LORD! How joyful are those who fear the LORD and delight in obeying his commands" (Psalm 112:1).

My response: Oh Father, how I love that the result of fearing You—giving You honor, exalting You, knowing You are great and we are small—results in joy! Your commands are for our good and bring us genuine delight! I'm so thankful I am Your child.

Additional Study Options:

What did you learn about God from Psalm 112? Add to your list in the Study Notes section at the back of this book or in your own journal.

Read All the Psalms Plan: Read Psalms 113-115.

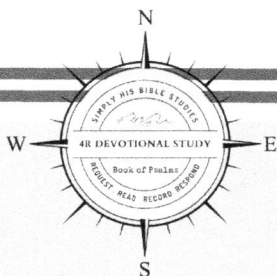

Psalm 116

Request: Heavenly Father, help me stay close to You, obeying Your commands and not straying from Your side. I want to be near You always. Please show me truths from Your Word as I listen and read. In Jesus' Name, Amen.

Read: Psalm 116

Record: Write down one verse from this passage that stood out to you.

Respond: Write a short prayer, talking to God about that verse.

Psalm 116 deals with an event that we will all face at some point unless Jesus returns first. We all had a birth day, and we will all have a death day. If we aren't believers in the Lord Jesus, saved by His grace, that is a scary sentence. However, if you have asked the Lord to forgive your sins and bowed to Him as Savior and Lord, you do not have to fear death at all. Not one little bit. When Jesus died on the cross, taking our punishment on Himself for all the sins we committed, He also conquered death itself. He walked out of the grave and now offers eternal life to all who follow Him. Wow. That is the very good news that Christians believe and share with those willing to listen.

Our psalmist had a near-death experience. We don't know what almost took his life. What we do know is that he did not want to die, and God rescued him from death at the time. The rescue was so miraculous that he is nearly trembling with gratitude. He praises God and wants to honor Him by telling us all about this rescue. He's determined to follow God wholeheartedly for the rest of his life, gratefully fulfilling his "vows to the LORD in the presence of all his people—in the house of the LORD . . . "(Psalm 116:18b-19a). He makes two statements I'd like to focus on with you.

First, he determines to pray for the rest of his life. The New Living Translation has a very poetic rendering of Psalm 116:2: "Because he bends down to listen, I will pray as long as I have breath!" Isn't that beautiful? God hears us. He hears the first lisping prayer of a toddler, the last whispered prayer of a dying saint, and everything in between! What a privilege we have. The God of the universe bends down to listen to us. Like a doting parent, He leans in to hear every word, every prayer, all our lives. I love that no matter how feeble I may become, I can do the work of prayer. I will be able to serve Him even in extreme weakness, interceding for others and praising Him. That warms my soul.

Second, our psalmist learned something else from this experience. I like the New International Version best for Psalm 116:15: "Precious in the sight of the Lord is the death of his faithful servants." When a faithful servant comes to the point of death, it's precious and valuable to our God. Why? Well, when our spirit slips out of a failing earthly body, it enters God's heavenly realm and is clothed in an immortal body. When we die, we finally begin to live without the shadow of sin and deception that abounds in this world. We see Jesus. What was once murky becomes clear. God is so excited about our living with Him that He went ahead to prepare a place for us there. (John 14:2-3)

You and I will be noticed when we die by God Almighty, and our death will be precious in His sight. A Christian never dies alone. No. God ushers us into His Presence with joy! Oh, how blessed we are. I think one of the most powerful testimonies Christians can give is to die with eagerness, knowing God is there to take us home. I really hope I will see His face (like Stephen, the first martyr, did) as I cross over from death to eternal life with Him. Wouldn't that be something? Let's live well here on earth, as long as He gives us breath, serving Him in whatever capacity we can. And when it's time to die, let's reach for His Abba-hand and joyfully enter the Kingdom He has prepared for those who love Him!

My verse: "The LORD cares deeply when his loved ones die" (Psalm 116:15).

My response: Lord, You noticed me from the moment of conception when I was being formed in the womb. You care deeply about the day of my death, as well. You number all my days in between. I'm so thankful for Your loving watch care over me all the days of my life and, then, forevermore!

Additional Study Options:

What did you learn about God from Psalm 116? Add to your list in the Study Notes section at the back of this book or in your own journal.

Read All the Psalms Plan: Read Psalms 117-118.

We have an enemy. Peter calls him a lion prowling about looking for someone to devour. (1 Peter 5:8) Paul warns us to armor up: "For our struggle is not against flesh and blood, but against the rulers, against the authorities, against the powers of this dark world and against the spiritual forces of evil in the heavenly realms" (Ephesians 6:12 NIV). Why am I talking about the evil one? Because he is actively roaming about, attempting to take a good thing—meeting with God daily—and twist it into a bad thing. Let's look at some of his deceptions and how we can combat them.

Condemnation. (Romans 8:1) The devil is great at condemning us when we fail. If we neglect our quiet time, he will do his best to make us feel worthless and inadequate. Your enemy will want you to give up. However, Paul says, "Therefore, there is now no condemnation for those who are in Christ Jesus" (Romans 8:1 NIV). Instead, listen to what Solomon says in Proverbs: "The godly may trip seven times, but they will get up again. But one disaster is enough to overthrow the wicked" (Proverbs 24:16). Just get back up and try again. God is delighted with every baby step we make toward consistency.

Accusation. (Revelation 12:10) The devil is also called the accuser in Scripture. He'll accuse you of having a quiet time to "look good." He'll tell you that you are being a legalist, trying to work your way to heaven. He'll accuse you of neglecting your family because you are taking time out to be with the Lord. Watch out for those kinds of accusations. The truth is, God loves you just as much whether you have a quiet time or not. We don't do it to earn His favor. *We do it because we need it, and we actually get to be with God.* It's a privilege to meet with Him, and it makes our hearts glad! God loves us and wants to show us how to live wisely. When we meet with Him and learn from Him, we are better equipped to bless those around us.

Lies. (John 8:44) The devil will tell you that if you don't feel like doing your quiet time, it won't be sincere. It would be better not to do it unless your mood is right. That's a lie. We create good habits despite our contrary emotions, don't we? I don't have to feel like brushing my teeth each night in order to brush them. Good hygiene dictates I do it no matter how I feel. Meeting with God often feels like a chore until we are actually seated and doing it. That tug to neglect the Word is straight from the enemy. When we ask for God's help? He makes the time sweet. Whether you feel like it or not, choose to meet with the Lord. You'll be so glad you did!

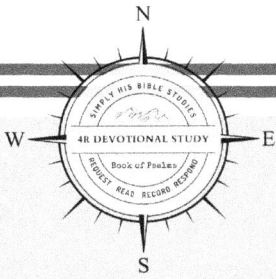

Psalm 119:1-56

Request: Father, help me to gain a greater appreciation for Your Word today. Thank You that I have the ability to read this psalm. Teach me, Lord, as I read. In Jesus' Name, Amen.

Read: Psalm 119:1-56

Record: Write down one verse from this passage that stood out to you.

Respond: Write a short prayer, talking to God about that verse.

Let's start by acknowledging that Psalm 119 is . . . long! In fact, it's the longest chapter in the entire Bible. Its purpose is to honor God's words to us in Scripture and express how important they are. The psalmist uses many different Hebrew words throughout this psalm to describe how God speaks to us. These words include law, judgments, testimonies, commandments, statutes, and precepts. In addition, this psalm is cleverly arranged, perhaps to make it easier to memorize. There are 22 sections in it, and each one is based on a letter of the Hebrew alphabet. (If we were doing this in English, there would need to be 26 sections based on our alphabet.) Each section has eight verses, and each verse starts with a word that begins with the Hebrew letter of that section. It's times like these when I wish I could read Hebrew!

Psalm 119 starts with the word "joyful" in my translation. Reading and obeying God's actual words written to us is a joyful, awe-inspiring exercise. When we study His Word and follow His directions, we walk more wisely and make better decisions. We learn not to compromise with evil but to choose wholesome, good paths. We read that those choices actually bring us great joy rather than feeling restrictive and limiting. Isn't that lovely?

Starting at verse four, we move from statements about God's words to prayer. The rest of the psalm is written in the form of a prayer addressed to God Himself. We are to read this psalm as a prayer. As we pray it, we are asking God to help us remember the words, "hiding" them in our hearts so we know how to behave in various situations. We are praying for open eyes to see the wonderful truths in His Word. In verse 35, our psalmist gets even more direct. "Make me walk along the path of your commands," he requests. (Psalm 119:35a, emphasis mine) He does not want to stray at all from doing what leads to a fulfilled and purposeful life.

Not only will God's words help us, they will actually give us freedom. Let's end with that thought today. "I will walk in freedom, for I have devoted myself to your commandments" (Psalm 119:45). Isn't that fascinating? Normally, we tend to think of commands as restrictive. However, we really gain freedom when we make good choices. We aren't skulking about trying to cover up sins and lies. We are free to fulfill the purpose God has marked out for us if we are walking the good path. Let's walk in freedom and joy by spending time each day soaking up and obeying God's words to us in the Bible!

My verse: "Make me walk along the path of your commands, for that is where my happiness is found" (Psalm 119:35).

My response: My happiness is found in You, Lord. Help me to walk in the paths of Your choosing, obeying Your commands that lead to great joy. I love that Your commands are not only for my good, but also for the good of others. You alone can help me choose rightly. Keep me close to You!

Additional Study Options:

What did you learn about God from Psalm 119:1-56? Add to your list in the Study Notes section at the back of this book or in your own journal.

Read All the Psalms Plan: Read Psalm 120.

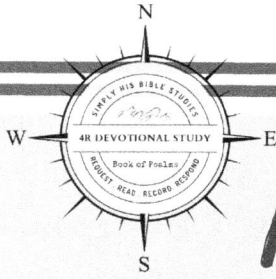

Psalm 119:57-112

Request: Lord God, I pray from this psalm today. "Open my eyes to see the wonderful truths in your instructions" (Psalm 119:18). In Jesus' Name, Amen.

Read: Psalm 119:57-112

Record: Write down one verse from this passage that stood out to you.

Respond: Write a short prayer, talking to God about that verse.

Do you have certain phrases locked in your brain because someone repeated them so often? I do. One of my favorite phrases is what my father-in-law would say whenever he didn't understand a person. Whether the person had hurt him or merely puzzled him, his standard response to me was, "People are funny, honey." He'd not only say it when he had his own troubles with people, he'd remind me of it when I shared my people issues, as well. That little, gentle phrase has stuck in my mind all these years. It's enabled me to accept others' quirks with more grace, believing the best about them instead of the worst.

Words, when repeated, stick. We are in the middle of a long list of reasons why the study of God's Word matters. Let's let the words wash over us and stick so that we value the treasure trove we have in the Bible. Here are some selected favorites from this next section of Psalm 119 that I'd like to meditate on with you today.

"I pondered the direction of my life, and I turned to follow your laws" (Psalm 119:59). Ponder. It means to think about something diligently, turning it over in one's mind. When I ponder my life and how I want it to unfold, I truly do turn to God's laws and His ways. I know they are best. At the end of my life, I want to look back and be grateful for the times I yielded to God's ways and followed His paths. We will be moving in the right direction if we walk in accordance with God's laws.

"You made me; you created me. Now give me the sense to follow your commands" (Psalm 119:73). This one made me chuckle. I need God to give me the good sense to do what is right! As my Creator, He knows me inside and out and can best guide me and help me choose wisely. Oh, how we need Him to give us the "smarts" to obey! That's where the Holy Spirit's fruit of self-control is such a gift to us—God's Spirit living in us, enabling us to do right.

"Your faithfulness extends to every generation, as enduring as the earth you created" (Psalm 119:90). What a lovely reminder right here in the middle of Psalm 119. Our God, who gave us good rules for living, is faithful. Always. He was faithful to the one who wrote this psalm. He is faithful to you and me. He will remain faithful to our grandchildren's grandchildren as they walk with Him! As the earth has endured for thousands of years, so will God's faithfulness. Rejoice!

These verses make me smile. They're like a sip of hot cocoa on a cold night, reminding me of the sweetness of following Him. They aren't necessarily new revelations. Instead, they comfort me with their consistent refrain, and I drink them up with a contented sigh. I am safe with the One who made me and who teaches me how best to live.

My verse: "My life constantly hangs in the balance, but I will not stop obeying your instructions" (Psalm 119:109).

My response: Oh Father, life is so precarious! Help me in the rough times as well as the sweet times to obey Your instructions, believing that they are right and good all the time.

Additional Study Options:

What did you learn about God from Psalm 119:57-112? Add to your list in the Study Notes section at the back of this book or in your own journal.

Read All the Psalms Plan: Read Psalm 122.

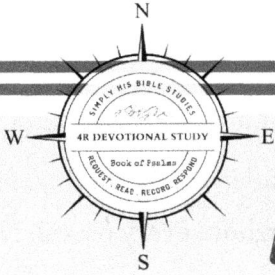

Psalm 119:113-176

Request: Thank You, Father, for Your good instructions. Show me today what You want me to see in Your Word and help me to carry it with me all day long. In Jesus' Name, Amen.

Read: Psalm 119:113-176

Record: Write down one verse from this passage that stood out to you.

Respond: Write a short prayer, talking to God about that verse.

_____

_____

_____

_____

_____

_____

_____

_____

One of the larger themes in this last section of Psalm 119 is the theme of the need for rescue. Our psalmist has many enemies. He's being oppressed and attacked. He's undergoing suffering. He cries out for rescue and continues to hold on to God's commands throughout every ordeal. No matter what, he wants to cling to what God says in His Word.

How about you and me? In troubled times, do we have that same passion to run to the Bible and the wisdom found there? Or are we fickle, often wanting to talk over our problems with our friends, seeking to be validated in our anger and hurt? I've been guilty of choosing to hash out offenses and grievances with others instead of bringing those hurts to the only One who can help me.

I can remember a difficult time in a church we attended where abuse had been uncovered. The church was rocked with the news that a man they had loved and trusted had abused several children over a period of time. It became the topic of every conversation for a season. I started to realize that I was no longer praying for that man or the families involved. I was endlessly talking about it. So, I made a commitment to the Lord: for every minute I spoke about this hard thing, I would pray about it for two minutes. This kept my conversations short and to the point. Talking about the trouble for half an hour meant I would need to spend an hour in prayer about it! Sadly, I realized I had fallen into the trap of gossip instead of doing the much needed work of prayer for our church and the hurting families.

We need to come to God first with our troubles. It's not wrong to seek godly counsel, but it is wrong to talk about our enemies over and over without bringing them to the Lord in prayer. He is the One who can help us—and them. We must be determined, like the psalmist, to spend our days meditating on God's Word. Then we will find ourselves at peace with the wisdom we need for every situation. Let's bring our troubles to the Lord, seeking His heart for us. It's only then that we'll find the answers and direction for our next steps.

My verse: "My eyes strain to see your rescue, to see the truth of your promise fulfilled" (Psalm 119:123).

My response: Help me, Lord, to wait with this kind of expectancy, knowing Your rescue will come as I look for You in the present darkness. Give me the sure hope this psalmist has—that all Your promises will be fulfilled even as I wait to see the rescue that is surely on its way!

Additional Study Options:

What did you learn about God from Psalm 119:113-176? Add to your list in the Study Notes section at the back of this book or in your own journal.

Read All the Psalms Plan: Read Psalm 123.

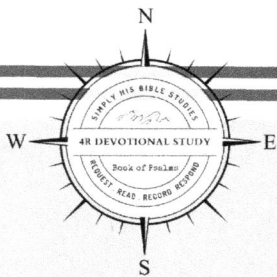

Psalm 121

Request: Father, as I start a new week of studying Your songbook, the Psalms, would you please give me joy and focus as I study? I love meeting with You. Help me to know You better because of this time with You and to love You more and more. In Jesus' Name, Amen.

Read: Psalm 121

Record: Write down one verse from this passage that stood out to you.

Respond: Write a short prayer, talking to God about that verse.

Let's pause to note that we are now in the section of the Book of Psalms that is known as the Songs of Ascent. Psalms 120-134 have a special place in Israel's "songbook." These fifteen psalms were to be sung by pilgrims climbing up toward Jerusalem for one of three festivals each year. Three times a year, those who were able made the trek to Jerusalem to celebrate a major holy day. As they climbed, they sang. Just like we sing certain songs at Christmas and Easter, these were their special songs. Can you imagine the beauty of thousands of faithful Jews flooding into Jerusalem to celebrate the LORD God together while singing praises? Keep this in mind as we read a selection from these special psalms.

When I was a little girl, my parents helped me memorize a few of the psalms. Psalm 121 is one of them. It's a beautiful psalm for someone who wants to be reminded that God watches over His own. I can remember reciting those beautiful words in my mind and feeling the comfort of them. "Behold, He that keepeth Israel neither slumbers nor sleeps" (Psalm 121:4 KJV). Yes, we memorized using the King James Version back in the day! What a blessing even that one line was for me. When I awakened from a nightmare or when sleep would not come, that little phrase from Psalm 121 reminded me that God was right there with me—wide awake and watching over me.

I love how this psalm begins with a question. Where does my help come from? That's of primary importance, isn't it? We can look for help in so many wrong places. We can watch a television show with an "expert." We can enjoy a YouTube video and glean advice there. Our next-door neighbor would probably gladly weigh in on where to go for help. While these answers won't necessarily be wrong, they might be. There's only one sure Source of help, and that is the Lord.

We need to weigh every bit of advice through the lens of His Word. When in trouble, let's start with Him! He will also lead us to those who can help us if we turn to Him first.

In my translation of this psalm, the word that is repeated is **watch**. God watches over us all our days, standing beside us in the day and in the night, close enough to shade us from harmful things. I love that I am never alone! Even when God allows a hard or painful experience into my life, I know it comes with purpose. (I think if I could see what He actually protects me from, I'd be amazed!) When hardships come, and they will, we can rest in knowing that God has allowed them and will keep watch with us through them. Troubles come to everyone. We who belong to Him, though, don't face them alone. Praise God for His watch care over us!

My verse(s): "The LORD himself watches over you! The LORD stands beside you as your protective shade" (Psalm 121:5).

My response: Holy God, what an astounding truth. You watch over me. I'm not just guarded by an angel (although that is amazing, too). Rather, I am watched over by You. You stand beside me, protective, steady, and sure. Thank You for this beautiful reassurance.

Additional Study Options:

What did you learn about God from Psalm 121? Add to your list in the Study Notes section at the back of this book or in your own journal.

Read All the Psalms Plan: Read Psalm 124.

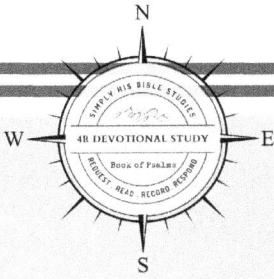

Psalm 126-127

Request: Lord, it's amazing to me that every time I sit to read Your Word, You are with me, as close as my next breath. Breathe life into me and show me Your light as I read, please. In Jesus' Name, Amen.

Read: Psalm 126-127

Record: Write down one verse from this passage that stood out to you.

Respond: Write a short prayer, talking to God about that verse.

As many of the Psalms of Ascent are short, we are going to read more than one each day. I love imagining the pilgrims choosing another song to help them huff and puff their way up to Jerusalem from the valley below! Let's take a look at two of these songs together.

Psalm 126 is a song of remembrance. There was a time when the Jewish people were exiled to Babylon and Assyria. Their land and their holy city of Jerusalem lay a barren wasteland. It was a time of great sorrow and grief for the Israelites. Miraculously, the day came when God allowed them to return once more to their homeland. The stories of Ezra and Nehemiah in the Old Testament chronicle the miraculous way God brought His people back. If you were ripped away from your homeland and not allowed to return for seventy years, you would never forget the day of your return. For most returning Israelites, they had only dreamed of Jerusalem. They were born in captivity and only heard the tales from those who had once lived there. It was like a dream to be able to go home again.

The message of the final two verses of Psalm 126 is also a message for us. There are times of weeping in everyone's life. During those times, we believe that we'll never experience joy again. The sadness seems too profound. And yet come it does. Joy returns after grieving, like spring returns after a long, hard winter. We can trust that principle, even when the winter is extra cold and raw. I'm so grateful for that!

Psalm 127 celebrates the family. Ponder what it must have been like for fathers and mothers to pack up their children and belongings and walk perhaps for several days to return to Jerusalem. This was no small task. Most of them camped in tents. Some stayed with relatives nearby. However, regular work had to stop. It was time to be together as a family and go on vacation! Don't you love that God mandated vacations three times a year by asking his people to return to

Jerusalem for the holy festivals? Makes me smile. One of my favorite verses in Psalm 127 is verse two. It serves as a reminder to busy parents then and now who perhaps find it hard to stop their work, fearing they will get behind. "It is useless for you to work so hard from early morning until late at night, anxiously working for food to eat; for God gives rest to his loved ones" (Psalm 127:2). We would all do well to remember that times of rest are important. We work better when we stop for a while to rejuvenate. Parents in all generations need to be reminded that their children are gifts to treasure. Those times of walking with family up to Jerusalem were important in building relationships and teaching the children God's truths. What a joyous song to sing on the way to a Jewish festival and what a timeless reminder for us today to value people (and especially our children) over endless work.

My verse: "Those who plant in tears will harvest with shouts of joy" (Psalm 126:5).

My response: Lord, I've seen this in my own lifetime over and over. Impossible, hopeless situations change, and despair is replaced with hope and joy. Help me to remember that life is not static. There are sad times and happy times. Yet in *all* the times, You are *always* working it *all* together for Your great good in my life.

Additional Study Options:

What did you learn about God from Psalms 126-127? Add to your list in the Study Notes section at the back of this book or in your own journal.

Read All the Psalms Plan: Read Psalms 125, 128.

Psalms 130, 131, 133

SIMPLY HIS BIBLE STUDIES

4R DEVOTIONAL STUDY

Book of Psalms

REQUEST READ RECORD RESPOND

Request: Teach me as I read today, Lord. Prepare me for the day ahead. In Jesus' Name, Amen.

Read: Psalms 130, 131, 133

Record: Write down one verse from this passage that stood out to you.

Respond: Write a short prayer, talking to God about that verse.

We are reading three short psalms today. I imagine they'd be easy to memorize. Perhaps they were some of the first songs of ascent that children would learn. They might have been sung several times to help the little ones remember them. Let's examine each one and learn from it.

Psalm 130 is a cry for help. It would give an Israelite words for times when they felt despair descend upon them. Part of this cry for help is an acknowledgment of guilt. We are all guilty of wrongdoing, and we all need God's forgiveness. The psalm rightly declares that without God's mercy, who can survive? Oh, how we need Him! The psalmist repeats himself in verse five. I imagine it to be a sort of chorus: "I am counting on the LORD; yes, I am counting on Him . . . " (Psalm 130:5a). What a beautiful song to memorize for times of panic and hopelessness.

Psalm 131 sounds more like a lullaby. It teaches an acceptance of God's superior wisdom and decision-making. He has the answers, and some of them are beyond our comprehension. This reminds me of God's own words to us in Isaiah 55:8-9 (NIV): "'For my thoughts are not your thoughts, neither are your ways my ways,' declares the Lord. 'As the heavens are higher than the earth, so are my ways higher than your ways and my thoughts than your thoughts.'" It's a humbling psalm. Let's be hushed and still before God, like a child who has been fully fed, trusting in the One who fed him.

Psalm 133 celebrates unity! How appropriate to sing on a pilgrimage as thousands of countrymen climb the steps to Jerusalem. What a joy it must have been to be a part of that crowd, all of whom had left their work and homes to worship together. Imagine how they would have been refreshed as they joined together for one purpose. As oil would feel on dry desert skin, so would the coming together of a nation to worship her King!

Each little psalm uniquely celebrates an aspect of being God's children. Each one would become dear to the Jewish people, being sung three times every year. I associate the hymn "Silent Night" with candles and church on Christmas Eve. It brings beautiful memories to mind of celebrating the birth of Jesus with my family. In the same way, these psalms must have brought joy to God's people, giving them enduring memories of worshiping together in Jerusalem.

My verse: "O Israel, hope in the LORD; for with the LORD there is unfailing love. His redemption overflows" (Psalm 130:7).

My response: My hope is in You, Lord! You do nothing stingily. Your love pours out without fail. Redemption flows and flows until it has filled the cup and spills over the sides. Your grace for us is incomprehensible. I treasure it.

Additional Study Options:

What did you learn about God from Psalms 130, 131, and 133? Add to your list in the Study Notes section at the back of this book or in your own journal.

Read All the Psalms Plan: Read Psalms 129, 132.

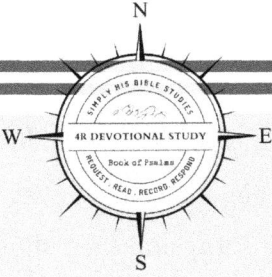

Psalm 136

Request: Heavenly Father, enable me to better comprehend the depth and width and height and length of Your love for me. It's unfathomable that You should love like You do. I am so grateful. In Jesus' Name, Amen.

Read: Psalm 136

Record: Write down one verse from this passage that stood out to you.

Respond: Write a short prayer, talking to God about that verse.

Psalm 136 is unique. It has 26 verses, repeating twenty-six times the phrase, "His faithful love endures forever." I really wish I could hear it sung. What did that refrain sound like? Was it chanted? Was it a catchy tune? Did they sing the first part of the verse softly and then shout out the chorus? As I read it, I can "hear" a kind of drum beat. After repeating, "His faithful love endures forever" over and over again, it might lodge in the brain and stay there. And that, of course, is the point.

We silly creatures can't quite wrap our minds around this amazing God who does not need us, but who wants us and loves us. In fact, He loves us so passionately that every book of the Bible proclaims it in various ways (just in case we missed the memo). We see His love in Genesis when He clothes the sinful Adam and Eve and continues to let them live after their failure. In fact, He whispers a promise to them even then that someday the serpent's head will be crushed. We see His love modeled by Joseph, who forgives the brothers who not only sold him into slavery, but almost murdered him. We see Boaz buy back Naomi's land and love his Ruth, showing us God's redeeming love. David pens the psalms that shout out God's shepherding love for us all. Hosea remarries an unfaithful woman, loving her back to himself, modeling what God has done countless times for His wayward people. We see it in Jesus' death and resurrection most of all, but also in Romans 8 and 1 Corinthians 13. Finally, we see it in Revelation 21:3-4 where God rejoices that His home is among His people and all wrongs will be made right.

God. Loves. You. (And me!) Please believe it. He really wants you to get this message solidly in your mind and in your heart.

Psalm 136 takes us to many diverse places that demonstrate God's love. The psalmist starts by reminding us that life itself is a miracle and creation shouts His love

for us. Among the planets, earth alone can sustain life. It's the exact distance it needs to be from the sun. The ecosystem works with rain falling and sun warming us. We read how God rescued His people from slavery in a mighty and frightening way and then brought them to the promised land. He sees us. He feeds us. He cares for us in our weakness. He vanquishes our enemies. This is our amazing God. Yes, His faithful love endures forever.

My verse: "He gives food to every living thing. *His faithful love endures forever*" (Psalm 136:25).

My response: I'm so grateful for the reminder that even little sparrows eat only because You give them food, Lord. All we have comes from You. You've been feeding Your creation now for thousands of years, replenishing the earth again and again. How awesome You are! Thank You.

Additional Study Options:

What did you learn about God from Psalm 136? Add to your list in the Study Notes section at the back of this book or in your own journal.

Read All the Psalms Plan: Read Psalms 134-135.

We are almost through our study. Can you believe it? I'm so glad you've stayed with it, reading God's Word each day, and seeking Him for His wisdom. I pray you've been blessed and changed as you've read and pondered each psalm. I hope this book becomes a treasure for you, too. It's filled with notes of your personal adventure with the Lord as He spoke to you through His Word, and you responded. It might be fun to keep and revisit it in the years ahead.

As you finish, be thinking about what you would like to study next. Perhaps you'll choose another book of the Bible to read, or you have a devotional book at the ready. Don't stop! The daily blessing of time with God changes us in beautiful ways.

Would you consider writing a review of this book on Amazon or Goodreads? Reviews help people decide whether a book is suitable for them. You could help them make that choice concerning this book. I'd greatly appreciate it. Also, I love hearing from readers. Feel free to email me anytime at Sharon@sweetselah.org. If you'd like to be put on the list for our weekly email newsletter, just ask! (I'll say yes.☺)

Well, it's time to turn to God's Word and listen for His voice as you read today. May He meet you this final week of our study in wonderful ways as you stop to be with Him!

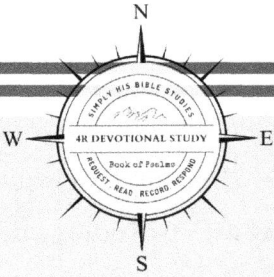

Psalm 139

Request: Father, today as I read in Psalm 139 how You carefully made me, help me to truly grasp how much You love me. Please open my eyes to see what You have for me in this psalm. In Jesus' Name, Amen.

Read: Psalm 139

Record: Write down one verse from this passage that stood out to you.

Respond: Write a short prayer, talking to God about that verse.

In this beautiful psalm, David celebrates that God is always with us. Let's look at just three of the ways this is true. First, God is with us wherever we go, wherever we are. This wonderful truth became so precious to me when Ray's military career took us to Germany with two little girls, a dog, and a cat. I felt so far away from my parents and friends back in New England. Then, Ray was re-assigned to Kuwait and fought in the Persian Gulf War. This psalm was such a comfort! God was with both me and Ray in these strange, new places, despite living oceans away from each other and from our families in Massachusetts. The specifics of Psalm 139 were reassuring and felt personal.

Second, God is with us no matter our age. He actually knew us before we were born and knit us together, creating a unique DNA pattern for each of us. He watched the delicate, inner parts of our bodies form and grow. He knew us before our parents realized we were there! And God has already recorded all our days in His Book of Life. He alone numbers our days, and we can trust that we will live out every one of them. Because of Jesus' death and resurrection, we can know Him forever, even after our spirits leave our earthly bodies, and when we are given new ones!

Third, God is with us inside and out. He knows our very thoughts. There is no place where we can hide from Him. All we are—the good, the bad, and the just plain ugly—is known to Him. Although this may make us uncomfortable, it should fill us with awe because it is true. Knowing every icky part of us, He still loves us enough to die for us. We can trust Him to search our hearts and test our thoughts. He will gently correct, forgive, or even applaud, always with the love of a good Shepherd, a tender Father, and a Savior.

My verse: "You see me when I travel and when I rest at home. You know everything I do" (Psalm 139:3).

My response: Father, what a sweet reminder for me during this busy season of speaking and travel. You see me in different hotels and retreat centers. You're with me wherever I go. You are my dear and constant Companion, my forever Abba who also calls me friend. Thank You!

Additional Study Options:

What do you learn about God from Psalm 139? Add to your list in the Study Notes section at the back of this book or in your own journal.

Read All the Psalms Plan: Read Psalm 137.

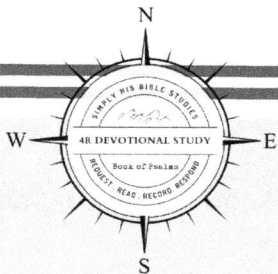

Psalm 140

Request: Lord, I pray along with David this morning, "Search me, O God, and know my heart; test me and know my anxious thoughts. See if there is any offensive way in me, and lead me in the way everlasting" (Psalm 139:23-24 NIV). In Jesus' Name, Amen.

Read: Psalm 140

Record: Write down one verse from this passage that stood out to you.

Respond: Write a short prayer, talking to God about that verse.

Psalm 140 is all about the wicked people of this world. David, sadly, had a lot of experience with people trying to harm him. For years, he was on the run from King Saul, who wanted to kill him. Many others in Israel would have loved to have killed him as well, to please Saul. David had to look around every corner before making a move. I am thankful to say that I can't relate to this way of living. How about you? Have you ever experienced that kind of hatred?

Whether or not we have personally experienced the animosity of others, we can relate to David's grief and the wicked desire to harm the innocent. Sometimes, the stories of violence feel too much to bear. We can certainly pray alongside David in asking that God rescue the poor and stop those who mean them harm.

What are some of the characteristics of the wicked as David describes them? They are violent. They are liars. They plot evil in their hearts. They don't try to calm troubled waters. Nope. They stir them up. They are vicious with their words. They actively try to trap others. If they succeed, they become prideful and even more wicked.

So, how do we reconcile David's cry for judgment to fall upon them with Jesus' command to love our enemies and pray for those who persecute us? We can pray for the wicked to repent and turn while still asking God to prevent them from hurting others. Let's do both. David ends his plea for a stop to evil by declaring his trust that someday God will, indeed, give justice to the poor. Let's also remember that there will be peace in God's presence for all who turn to Him in repentance, trust, and humility.

My verse: "But I know the LORD will help those they persecute; he will give justice to the poor" (Psalm 140:12).

My response: Lord, I'm so thankful You care when someone is denied justice and is persecuted. I'm so glad You are just and will not let evil go unpunished. Thank You that there will come a day when all will be made right. In this day, Lord, please come alongside and rescue those being harmed and cause the wicked among us to repent before it is too late.

Additional Study Options:

What did you learn about God from Psalm 140? Add to your list in the Study Notes section at the back of this book or in your own journal.

Read All the Psalms Plan: Read Psalm 138.

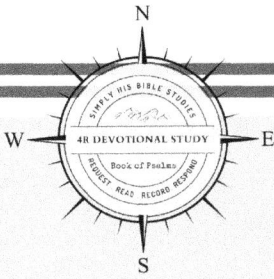

Psalm 143

Request: Father God, thank You for inviting me to come. You want me here, right now, opening Your Word and listening. Give me ears to hear! In Jesus' Name, Amen.

Read: Psalm 143

Record: Write down one verse from this passage that stood out to you.

Respond: Write a short prayer, talking to God about that verse.

This is a psalm for times of depression and anxiety. I love that David is honest with the Lord about his fears and his increasing desperation. I wonder if it was written while living in a cave during his years of hiding from Saul. Verse three seems to indicate this: "My enemy has chased me. He has knocked me to the ground and forces me to live in darkness like those in the grave" (Psalm 143:3). I don't know about you, but I might feel like David if I were living in a dark and gloomy cave with no way out. As I related previously, I too had a season of depression after the birth of my first daughter, while carrying my second daughter. I felt like I was in a cave mentally and emotionally. The world even looked dark and heavy.

So, let's learn some lessons from David. First, of course, is a lesson we've already learned as we've studied the Psalms. It's okay to honestly tell God how very unhappy we are. We don't need to hide it. We can cry out to Him and plead for help. Repeatedly. There are also things we can do to help lighten the darkness. They take effort, and I do remember that depression makes even the smallest effort seem herculean. Let's see what David did.

- He reminded himself that God was faithful and righteous. (vs. 1)
- He came in humility, knowing he was not innocent. No one is. (vs. 2)
- He remembers what God has done in the past. (vs. 5)
- He lifts his hands to God in prayer and yearns for God to come near. (vs. 6)
- He asks for assurance of God's unfailing love each morning and seeks God's guidance for the day. (vs. 8)
- He humbles himself, asking God to hide him, to teach him, to lead him onward. (vv. 9-10)
- He declares that God is *his* God. He is not alone, no matter how alone he feels. (vs. 10)

These are great reminders of what to do when the darkness crowds in, aren't they? If we can't quite come up with words as eloquent as David's, turn to Psalm 143 and read his. I believe that's one reason God has them in His living Word to us. When we don't know what to pray, we can come to these beautiful songs and pray from them. What a gift the Psalms are to us!

My verse: "Let me hear of your unfailing love each morning, for I am trusting you. Show me where to walk, for I give myself to you" (Psalm 143:8).

My response: Yes, please! I know I am always loved by You, but my daily quiet time reminders are so sweet. I do surrender to You and Your will for how I should walk today.

Additional Study Options:

What do you learn about God from Psalm 143? Add to your list in the Study Notes section at the back of this book or in your own journal.

Read All the Psalms Plan: Read Psalms 141-142.

Psalm 144

Request: Heavenly Father, I come to You needing Your guidance and a reminder that I am Yours. Always. Please speak as I listen and read. In Jesus' Name, Amen.

Read: Psalm 144

Record: Write down one verse from this passage that stood out to you.

Respond: Write a short prayer, talking to God about that verse.

Psalm 144 is a song for a nation to sing when its king and soldiers are armed for battle. The first time I read it, I imagined myself in Israel with a vicious enemy encircling my nation. I love that David gives God credit in every aspect of the battle. God is the one who trains his hands and gives his fingers skill. He is the one in charge of the nations, and David rightly looks to Him! It's a powerful song ending with a prayer for peace, a time when their enemies will no longer attempt to break through and capture God's people. David sings of a time when the barns are filled with crops and children flourish. Someday, when Jesus returns, this will be true. We can rejoice!

This psalm can also be used as a prayer by those of us doing battle on our knees, lifting to God loved ones who are under the attack by the enemy of their souls. Re-read this psalm, if you have time, from that perspective. God, who is our rock, arms us for battle as He helps us to pray, causing the Holy Spirit to move in our loved ones' lives. We can cry out to Him, "Open the heavens, LORD, and come down. Touch the mountains so they billow smoke.... Reach down from heaven and rescue..." (Psalm 144:5, 7a).

Let's pray from verse 12 that our sons "flourish in their youth" and that our daughters are full of grace. This psalm encourages us to pray for those within our family circle as well as others. Let's pray that the enemy will be unable to break through the walls of our loved ones and capture them. I've seen God move in miraculous ways when His people pray. Perhaps this beautiful psalm can be useful for you and me as we pray and ask God for victory in others' lives.

My verses: "Open the heavens, LORD, and come down. Touch the mountains so they billow smoke" (Psalm 144:5).

My response: Lord, there are days when I long for you to open the heavens and come down and reign in righteousness and truth. I long for a time when liars can't lie and Your people can live in peace. We weren't made for this corrupted world. We long for the new heaven and new earth to come. Maranatha! Come, Lord Jesus.

Additional Study Options:

What did you learn about God from Psalm 144? Add to your list in the Study Notes section at the back of this book or in your own journal.

Read All the Psalms Plan: Read Psalm 145.

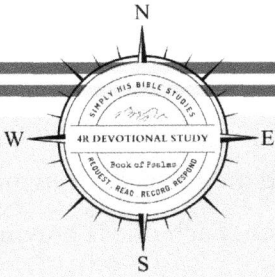

Psalm 146

Request: Thank You, Father, for caring about me, being with me and within me as I open Your living Word. Please teach me and touch me today. In Jesus' Name, Amen.

Read: Psalm 146

Record: Write down one verse from this passage that stood out to you.

Respond: Write a short prayer, talking to God about that verse.

_____

_____

_____

_____

_____

_____

_____

_____

In my living room, hung on either side of our fireplace mantel, are two pictures. They are not particularly fancy. I think my Aunt Nancy found them at a thrift store and then gave them to me. I love these pictures. One is of an old woman and the other of an old man. Each one is praying with a Bible opened and a bowl of soup on the table next to it. The woman also has a mug of water, and the man has a loaf of bread. Every time I look at these pictures, I'm reminded of what matters most: God Himself, Living Water, Bread of Life, in relationship with me. He's been my God since I chose to follow Him as a four-year-old. I want to be like that old man and woman. I want to be contented with spiritual food from the Word and grateful for physical food, no matter how simple.

Our psalm for today declares, "I will praise the LORD as long as I live. I will sing praises to my God with my dying breath" (Psalm 146:2). Yes, and Amen. May it be so. Words like these affirm for me my commitment to the Lord again. It's similar to the feeling I get when I sit next to my Ray at a wedding and as the bride and groom say their vows, I squeeze his hand and whisper, "Yes. I still do!" Hearing those pledges of faithfulness strengthens our commitment to each other.

We read and re-read the Bible because we need reminding. We can so easily drift away. Ancient words, reaffirming eternal truths, anchor us. This psalm does more than declare a faithful love for God, though. It also celebrates our wonderful God. He is our Creator and created every single thing. He cares for all people. God cares for the oppressed, the hungry, the imprisoned, the blind, and the weighed down. He notices and protects foreigners and immigrants, orphans and widows. And He loves the godly. Can you find yourself in this list? I can find me! There are times when I feel weighed down or shackled by some misfortune. There are days when I am just Sharon, counted among "the godly" because of God's grace through Jesus. Each one of us

is on this list. Even the wicked are there! God frustrates their plans and won't allow their plans to succeed forever. Sometimes the wicked repent and join the godly by the grace of God. Let's celebrate our great God today and ask Him for the endurance to declare our love for Him until our dying breath!

My verse: "The LORD opens the eyes of the blind. The LORD lifts up those who are weighed down. The LORD loves the godly" (Psalm 146:8).

My response: Thank You, Father, that You care for those with physical ailments like blindness and those with mental ailments like depression. Help those who struggle. Lift up those who feel weighed down. Thank You for Your forever love!

Additional Study Options:

What did you learn about God from Psalm 146? Add to your list in the Study Notes section at the back of this book or in your own journal.

Read All the Psalms Plan: Read Psalm 147.

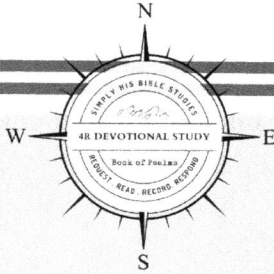

Psalm 148

Request: I'm so thankful, Lord, for these precious quiet moments with You. Thank You for loving me. In Jesus' Name, Amen.

Read: Psalm 148

Record: Write down one verse from this passage that stood out to you.

Respond: Write a short prayer, talking to God about that verse.

_____

_____

_____

_____

_____

_____

_____

_____

This is a psalm bursting with praise. The psalmist is so overcome with the desire to worship that he is recruiting everyone and everything to join him in worship! From angelic beings to "small scurrying animals and birds" (vs. 10), there's a clarion call for all creation to worship our great God. I don't know what the tune to this song was, but don't you think it must have been loud, rollicking, and a bit on the wild side? It's a delight to read.

The psalm begins in the heavens. We are reminded that there are created beings there whom most of us have yet to meet. Angels are such a mystery to me. What do they look like? How many tens of thousands *are* there, considering the Bible refers to them in terms of legions and armies? Despite how often the Bible refers to them, they remain a mystery. We know they do God's bidding. We know that some of them chose to follow Satan and left heaven. We know that they comfort people, warn people, and bring tidings of great joy. We also know that the first reaction most humans have when they encounter an angel is to drop to the ground in amazement and fear. How powerful, glorious, and awesome they must be!

These otherworldly beings, that would make my little legs tremble, all bow the knee to our magnificent God. Even the sun, moon, and stars were created by Him and owe Him their allegiance. One of the most astounding phrases in this psalm is found in verse 5: ". . . for he issued his command, and they came into being." God, the Word, spoke and galaxies appeared. No matter how big something is, He is bigger.

The psalm then moves from the heavens to the earth and describes living creatures of all shapes and sizes. All animals on earth, all creatures in the sea, all birds in the air owe Him their allegiance. So do we. Whether a tiny child or a great king, someday every knee will bow and honor the One who created him. Yet even this is not enough for the psalmist. He enlists the weather. How fun is that? The weather obeys Him and ought to bow before His authority. He then calls on the trees and mountains to worship God as well. He is diligent in including everything, isn't he?

Why should all creation worship God? We find the answer at the end of our psalm: "Let them all praise the name of the LORD. For his name is very great; his glory towers over the earth and heaven!" (Psalm 148:13) Let's join him in this chorus of praise today.

My verses: "Let every created thing give praise to the LORD, for he issued his command, and they came into being" (Psalm 148:5).

My response: You issued a command, making all of creation from nothing. How incredible! There is none like You! Too often we ignore You and fail to thank You for the gift of being alive. We only have breath because You gave it. Help me, Lord, to never lose the wonder of being given all this by You.

Additional Study Options:

What did you learn about God from Psalm 148? Add to your list in the Study Notes section at the back of this book or in your own journal.

Read All the Psalms Plan: Read Psalm 149.

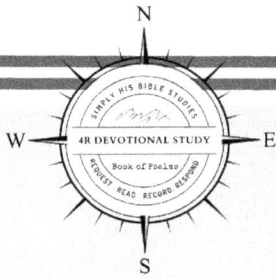

Psalm 150

Request: Heavenly Father, as I turn to the final psalm in this songbook, help me to glean any remaining thought, command, or desire You have for me. Thank You for this wonderful book of songs, dedicated to worshiping You and crying out to You from the heart. Thank You that I am held by You in every storm and situation. Keep me near. In Jesus' Name, Amen.

Read: Psalm 150

Record: Write down one verse from this passage that stood out to you.

Respond: Write a short prayer, talking to God about that verse.

Because I want to end with my commentary today, I've rearranged things a bit. You'll read my verse and my response next, as well as our additional options. Please do read my "last words" to you as we finish our study together. Thank you for joining me on this walk through the Psalms.

My verse: "Praise him with a clash of cymbals; praise him with loud clanging cymbals" (Psalm 150:5).

My response: I read this, Lord, and realize that perhaps I am more restrained than I should be in my praise. Help me not be afraid to occasionally roar with joy and overflowing praise, to shout until I'm hoarse out of loud love for You! I think of a football stadium where the crowd leaps to their feet in a thunderous shout of victory! Thank You for the reminder that it's okay to be noisy in my praise for You. And You are happy to receive quieter praise, too.

Additional Study Options:

What did you learn about God from Psalm 150? Add to your list in the Study Notes section at the back of this book or in your own journal.

Read All the Psalms Plan: Congratulations. You're done!

Such a short psalm to finish out this great big Book of Psalms! We've seen so many forms of writing in this songbook of the Jewish people. I'm thankful for the history lessons. Humbled by the psalmists who confessed sins so openly. Encouraged by the freedom the writers had to share all their doubts, anger, and frustrations with the Lord so honestly. Inspired by the depths of yearning to be near to Him. And delighted with the many ways we have to praise Him. How about you? I hope you've grown in your ability to come to God honestly, no matter what, knowing He will hold you close and listen, letting you be "you" in your rawest form. God loves you and me so very much. He truly is our safe place.

This last psalm calls for shouting, clanging, and dancing. It makes me think of King David when he entered Jerusalem with the ark. "And David danced before the LORD with all his might, wearing a priestly garment. So David and all the people of Israel brought up the Ark of the Lord with shouts of joy and the blowing of rams' horns" (2 Samuel 6:14-15). Sometimes, you just need to be loud!

This psalm isn't asking us to use only our voices. Our psalmist is calling all the musicians to join in this glorious worship with ram's horns, lyres, harps, tambourines, stringed instruments, flutes, and cymbals. This psalm describes a party. A holy, happy, God-focused party.

God sees us as individuals and wants us, with all our different temperaments, to come to Him. Some of us would be tapping lightly on a tambourine, happy to watch the dancers. Others would be boisterous in their praise. That, too, is actively encouraged in Psalm 150. God says, "Be still and know that I am God!" (Psalm 46:10a) We can also "praise him with loud clanging cymbals" (Psalm 150:5b). Either way is just fine with Him.

If there's one thing the Psalms have taught me, it's that I can come just as I am, knit together by my Creator the way He wanted me, and nestle in. Let me encourage you to be yourself with Him.

Be held and be grateful. You are loved.

GROUP STUDY

If you choose to do this study with a group, this section provides guidance, suggestions, and group study questions for each week.

Optional Group Study

Digging deeper into . . .

Held.

A Bible Study of the Book of Psalms

Dear Group Members: The goal of the book you are holding is that you, the reader, will meet with God individually, trust Him to show you truths from His Word, and spend time pondering what He teaches you. I want so much for you to experience the joy of daily time alone with Him, hearing from His Spirit as you study His Word with a listening heart. A group study is optional. This guide is for small groups who choose to band together to share and study further. These are not homework questions to add to your daily study. The questions in this guide are to be seen and studied in a group setting. Hopefully, they will help grow your understanding of the passages you've read during the week before. As you meet together, my prayer is that you learn more about each other, pray together for personal growth, and find rich truths and new discoveries by talking about God's Word. May God bless your group time mightily!

Dear Group Leaders: Your most important job as a leader is to pray for the group ahead of time. Ask the Lord to give you His wisdom and discernment, and then rely on His Spirit to lead and guide during the group times. The weekly lessons are designed to help you shepherd your group toward greater understanding of the passages read during the week and to help your group members apply what is learned to their daily lives. My heart's desire is that group meetings will be rich times of sharing and strengthening each other through fresh Bible reading, accountability, and prayer. God created us to be part of His body, growing through life's trials and helping one another along the way. Please don't feel you have to "finish" the questions each week. It would take an average group two hours of meeting time to answer all the questions. So, feel free to linger over questions when a need is felt, skipping questions as the Spirit leads. Your primary goal each week is to address the needs of your unique group. May God guide you as you love on each member and learn right along with your group just how much God loves you and how closely you are . . . *held*.

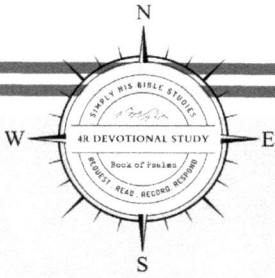

Introductory Meeting

Beginnings (20 minutes)

1. Open in prayer. Ask God to lead your study; ask that His Presence will be felt, and His Name lifted high.

2. If you or your church has purchased the books, pass them out to all attendees. Remind each attendee that they should bring their book, a Bible, and a pen to each class. (Be very kind to those who forgot and have extra books/Bibles/pens available!)

3. Spend some time getting to know each other with simple questions (name, where they're from, have they ever studied the Psalms, etcetera).

Quiet Time (20 minutes)

1. Read Psalm 3 silently at least two times.

2. Choose a favorite verse that intrigues, inspires, or perhaps confuses you, and write it out here:

3. Go around the circle and share your verse. If it's not too personal, we'd love to know why you selected this verse. How did God speak to you through it?

Group Discussion (30-45 minutes)

Read 2 Samuel 15. It's the back story on the history of the writing of Psalm 3.

1. What did Absalom do to win the favor of the people?

2. By the time David was made aware of Absalom's deceit, it was too late to stop him. Instead, David left Jerusalem. Why do you think David missed all that was happening with Absalom?

3. What were David's concerns when he left the city?

4. David sent the Ark of God back to the city (vv. 25-29). Discuss his reasoning and apply it to life today. Can we receive what God decides with good grace like David did?

5. David wept, barefoot, and with head covered. What can we learn about emotions from David? Is it hard for you to weep with others as he did? How does our culture affect our ability to show emotion?

6. When a child turns against a parent, the pain feels intolerable. How would you advise and encourage a parent in that situation? What Bible verses do you think might help? When is sitting in silence and simply grieving the better answer?

7. Now read Psalm 3 once more. What do you see there after studying 2 Samuel 15 that you might have missed before?

8. The Book of Psalms will teach us how to praise God exuberantly and how to lament with raw and honest emotion. It will teach us lessons on how to live as well as remind us of the great things God has done. What are you most eager to learn?

Assignment for the Coming Week

1. Read Days 1-7 this week.

2. Make sure you write out your verse and response each day.

3. Review all seven days and choose the day and verse that stood out to you the most. Come prepared to share that verse with your class next week.

Note: Each week at this group time, after you share your favorite verses of the week, you will work as a class to answer various questions together that tie in with the previous week's study. You are not expected to have answers to group discussion questions prepared in advance. Your focus during the week should be to meet with God each day, discover "your verse," and write your response. The group study questions are to be answered as a group when you are together.

Close in prayer.

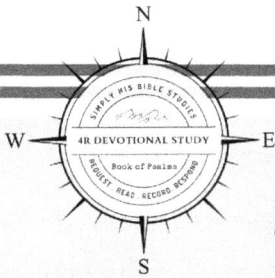

Week One Group Study

Come prepared to discuss the readings listed for Days 1-7.

Open in prayer.

1. Start by sharing with each other a favorite verse from your readings this past week. Talk about why it "mattered" to you and, if willing, share your response to the Lord about the verse.

2. There are many different types of psalms in the Book of Psalms. I've identified nine types. We'll look at a different type each week as part of our Bible Study. You've already experienced quite a variety in Week One. Here's our list:

   - Wisdom—advice on how to live wisely (Psalm 1)
   - Lament—anguished cries in troubled times (Psalm 5)
   - Praise—praise for who God is (Psalms 8 and 16)
   - Imprecatory—anger toward enemies (Psalm 10)
   - History—rooted in historical events (Psalms 11 and 18)
   - Ascent—specifically sung when climbing up to Jerusalem for festivals
   - Thanksgiving—gratitude for what God has done
   - Royal—for the kings of Israel
   - Songs of Zion—specific to Israel (songs of captivity, Jerusalem, the land of Israel)

   Why do you think there are so many different types of psalms? What do you think is the purpose of each? As you read, watch for the different kinds and see if you agree with me. Perhaps you'll find another category or two to add to this list!

Today, we will focus on Psalm 1, a Wisdom Psalm. Mirriam Jolie defines a Wisdom Psalm this way: "Wisdom psalms are psalms that reflect on Wisdom, the law of God, and the fate of the wicked and the righteous. They teach believers to fix their minds and hearts on the truly ultimate things rather than living for short-term gain." (https://christianfaithguide.com/what-are-wisdom-psalms/)

3. The first verse of Psalm 1 is full of warnings. Give an example from today of what following the advice of the wicked might look like. What would standing around with sinners look like? What is a mocker, and what are some examples of mocking you see in our culture?

4. The verses in Psalm 1:2-3 are at the heart of our study. It's why we are seeking to read the Word daily. Talk together about good patterns and rhythms a Christian might develop in order to delight in the Bible and meditate on it "day and night." What does that look like, practically, for busy women? Why do you think the psalmist used a tree by a river as an illustration for the godly person?

5. Finish looking at Psalm 1 by comparing and contrasting those who love God's Word with those who don't. What is the difference between a tree planted by a river and chaff? What *is* chaff?

6. Look back at the list of types of psalms. Which one intrigues you the most? Why?

7. What were the obstacles you faced during Week One that made it harder for you to meet with God? How can you overcome them?

8. Share the "place" where you meet with God with one another. Do you sit in your living room? Hide in the bathroom? Are you on your porch? Talk about the importance of a special place set apart for Bible time. Do you think the place you choose matters? Why or why not?

Assignment for the coming week: Read Days 8 through 14, and write out your verse and response each day. Review all your responses before the next study, and choose which verse and response you'd like to share with the group.

Close in prayer.

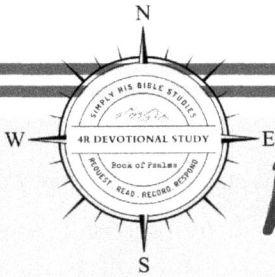

Come prepared to discuss the readings listed for Days 8-14.

Open in prayer.

1. Start by sharing with each other a favorite verse from your readings this past week. Talk about why it "mattered" to you and, if willing, share your response to the Lord about the verse.

2. This week, we are going to focus on a Praise Psalm. When we praise God, we are celebrating who He is, His characteristics. Take a moment as a group, and talk about some of your favorite attributes of God. See how many you can list. I'll get you started: He's the Alpha and Omega—the first and the last. He's merciful. He's omnipresent. Have fun celebrating this wonderful, unique King of kings, Sovereign God, the One who loves you.

3. In Psalm 23, David focuses on God's attributes by comparing God to a good shepherd. Let's start by reading about David's life as a shepherd. Read these passages out loud together: 1 Samuel 16:6-13 and 1 Samuel 17:32-49.

4. Next, read Psalm 23 out loud. What do you learn about God from these verses?

5. The first three verses describe what a good shepherd does to care for his sheep. He makes them lie down in green pastures. He leads them beside quiet waters. It's clear God values times of rest for His people. How do these times of quiet restore a soul and guide us to paths of righteousness?

6. Do you find it hard to rest? Why or why not? Do you think American culture makes it easy or difficult to rest? What's the difference between intentional rest and laziness or sloth?

7. Describe what it would look like to have God with you while walking in the valley of the shadow of death. How can we remember that God is with us in the hard times?

8. What does it mean to have a table prepared in the presence of enemies?

9. We don't anoint heads with oil very often anymore. In a dry climate, the moistness of oil on a parched face would feel so good, wouldn't it? How does God anoint us today and help our cups to overflow?

10. Psalm 23:6 gives us great assurance. What do you look forward to when you think of passing from this earth to heaven as a child of God?

Assignment for the coming week: Read Days 15-21, and write out your verse and response each day. Review all your responses before the next study, and choose which verse and response you'd like to share with the group.

Close in prayer. Praying scripture is a sweet method of planting His Word in our hearts. Consider closing in prayer using Psalm 23 as a guide.

LORD God, thank You that You are our Shepherd, and because of Your care, we have all we need. Help us to obey You when You make us lie down in rest, and lead us to quiet places. Restore our souls. Guide us in paths of righteousness for Your great name's sake. Remind us that You never leave us, even when we are walking in the shadow of death. With You beside us, we do not need to fear evil. Comfort us with Your rod and staff. Help us to sit down and eat at the table You prepare even when we are surrounded by enemies. Anoint us with Your Holy Spirit until our cups overflow! Surely, Your goodness and mercy will follow us all the days of our lives. We look forward to the day we will dwell in Your house forever. We worship You, Shepherd of our souls. In Jesus' Name, Amen.

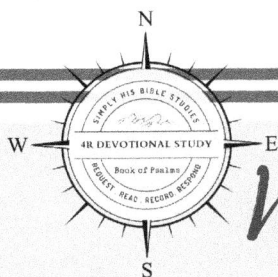

Week Three Group Study

Come prepared to discuss the readings listed for Days 15-21.

Open in prayer.

1. Start by sharing with each other a favorite verse from your readings this past week. Talk about why it "mattered" to you and, if willing, share your response to the Lord about that verse.

2. Read Psalm 42, a Lament Psalm, out loud together.

3. This psalm was written by "the sons of Korah." Korah was not a hero. Read a summary of his story in Numbers 26:7-11. (The longer version of this story is found in Numbers 16.) What did Korah do, according to Numbers 26:9? Why do you think the line of Korah was not wiped out (Numbers 26:11)?

4. The descendants of Korah redeemed themselves in future generations. Read 1 Chronicles 9:19-21. What was their responsibility? Read 1 Chronicles 15:16-18. In verse 18, what do we learn that they did? Lastly, what was their role in 1 Chronicles 12:6?

5. Read Psalm 42:3, 9-10. What emotions is the writer of this psalm experiencing? Why do you think God wants us to read psalms of lament?

6. Psalm 42 not only contains lament; it also contains hope. What can we learn from the psalmist about how to wrestle with depression and anguish in our thought lives?

7. Read the "chorus" of this psalm in verses 5 and 11. The psalmist is giving himself a

"pep talk." Have you ever done that? What are some truths you could tell yourself during a season of bleakness?

8. Read Psalm 42:1. Why is the psalmist thirsting for God? How does God fill and satisfy us?

9. Discuss our culture and the ways we lament. Think about funerals and the way we grieve in America. Compare it to how the psalmist grieved. Are we too restrained?

10. How can we help someone lament well while guarding against debilitating and crippling self-pity?

Assignment for the coming week: Read Days 22-28, and write out your verse and response each day. Review all your responses before the next study, and choose which verse and response you'd like to share with the group.

Close in prayer.

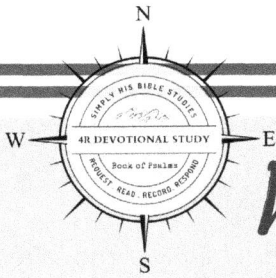

Come prepared to discuss the readings listed for Days 22-28.

Open in prayer.

1. Start by sharing with each other a favorite verse from your readings this past week. Talk about why it "mattered" to you and, if willing, share your response to the Lord about the verse.

2. Psalm 51, a History Psalm, describes when Nathan the prophet came to David after he had committed adultery with Bathsheba. The story is found in 2 Samuel 11. Ask someone in your group to summarize David's sins.

3. Now, read together Nathan's rebuke in 2 Samuel 12:1-25. How did Nathan "get through" to David and break the hardness of heart in the king?

4. What were the consequences of David's sin?

5. How did David respond to the consequences?

6. Now, read Psalm 51. This likely took place after Nathan came to David but before his first child by Bathsheba died. What do we learn about deep repentance from this psalm?

7. Why is it hard for us to confess sin?

8. Read 1 John 1:8-10. What do we learn about confession in this passage? Which is

harder: to forgive others who have sinned against us but repented, or to forgive ourselves after we've repented?

9. Read Psalm 103:8-14. What do we learn from this passage about God's response to us when we've sinned?

10. Discuss what happens when we don't confess sin. How does it harm us and others when sins remain hidden?

Assignment for the coming week: Read Days 29-35, and write out your verse and response each day. Review all your responses before the next study, and choose which verse and response you'd like to share with the group.

Close in prayer.

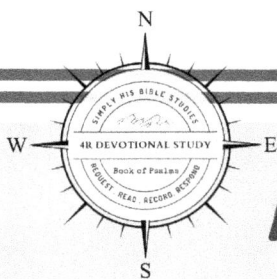

Week Five Group Study

Come prepared to discuss the readings listed for Days 29-35.

Open in prayer.

1. Start by sharing with each other a favorite verse from your readings this past week. Talk about why it "mattered" to you and, if willing, share your response to the Lord about the verse.

2. This week, our focus will be the Songs of Zion. While these songs are specific to the nation of Israel, we can still learn from them. Read Psalm 74.

3. What do you learn about the history of the Jewish nation from this psalm?

4. What is the complaint or lament of this psalm?

5. Have you ever felt abandoned by God? What can you glean from this psalm to help you or a friend better face that feeling?

6. This psalm was written by a man named Asaph. He wrote twelve of the psalms in the Book of Psalms and, therefore, deserves some attention. What do you learn about Asaph in the following passages: 1 Chronicles 6:31-32 and 39; 1 Chronicles 16:1-5; 2 Chronicles 29:30?

7. Read Psalm 79:1-5. This psalm, written by Asaph, is a psalm of lament over the destruction of the temple before the temple had even been built. This puzzled me when I

first realized Asaph lived in David's day before the temple. Then I read 2 Chronicles 29:30 and realized he was a seer. What must it have been like for Asaph to see such a devastating future? Would you have wanted his job? How would Psalm 79 have comforted the Israelites after the temple was destroyed? After it was rebuilt and they returned from Babylon? What do you think its purpose is?

8. Take some time to talk about your daily study of the Psalms. What type of psalms resonate most with you? Have they changed your prayer life at all? If so, how?

9. Has anything surprised you about the Psalms? Did you expect the variety of themes and emotions found within them? Has anything disturbed you as you've read?

Assignment for the coming week: Read Days 36-42, and write out your verse and response each day. Review all your responses before the next study, and choose which verse and response you'd like to share with the group.

Close in prayer.

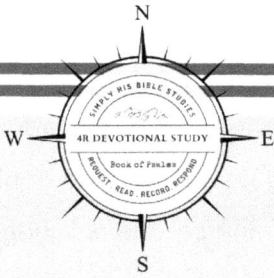

Week Six Group Study

Come prepared to discuss the readings listed for Days 36-42.

Open in prayer.

1. Start by sharing with each other a favorite verse from your readings this past week. Talk about why it "mattered" to you and, if willing, share your response to the Lord about the verse.

2. Our focus this week is a Thanksgiving Psalm. The Bible is full of reminders for us to be grateful. Read Psalm 7:17, Psalm 100:4, Luke 17:11-19, Philippians 4:6, Colossians 3:15-17, 1 Thessalonians 5:18, and Hebrews 12:28. What do you learn about being thankful from these verses?

3. Read Psalm 95 together and list all the things the psalmist is thankful for.

4. Take some time as a group to list things you are thankful for today. Here are some thoughts to get you started: Did you have hot water for your shower this morning? Did you have drinkable water from your faucet? Do you have a roof over your head? There's sooo much to be grateful for when we start counting our blessings!

5. Let's spend some time on the only psalm in the Bible written by Moses, Psalm 90. Read the psalm out loud together.

6. Moses speaks a lot in this psalm about the brevity of life. Have you found that to be true? How is it helpful to remember this?

7. What are some ways you are "numbering your days"—trying to live for what matters?

8. We're going to finish our time with the only psalm in the Bible that is miserable from beginning to end—Psalm 88. You may not have time to read it, but let's talk about its content. It was written by Heman, a contemporary of King David, and one of his songwriters and musicians. Heman was also the grandson of Samuel, the last judge of Israel. (See 1 Chronicles 6:33.) Why do you think a psalm with no happy ending is included in the Book of Psalms?

9. Psalm 88 begins, "LORD, you are the God who saves me; day and night I cry out to you" (Psalm 88:1 NIV). Heman's sadness and grief were not taken away, yet he continues to cry out. What does that teach us about coming to God in times of darkness? How do you think Samuel's legacy of faithfully serving God might have influenced his grandson, Heman?

10. Let's return to our thanksgiving theme. How can being grateful help us in the dark times?

Assignment for the coming week: Read Days 43-49, and write out your verse and response each day. Review all your responses before the next study, and choose which verse and response you'd like to share with the group.

Close in prayer.

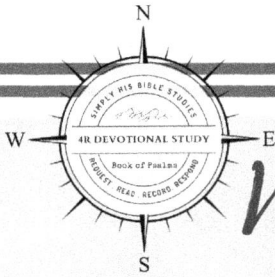

Week Seven Group Study

Come prepared to discuss the readings listed for Days 43-49.

Open in prayer.

1. Start by sharing with each other a favorite verse from your readings this past week. Talk about why it "mattered" to you and, if willing, share your response to the Lord about the verse.

2. Let's look at a Royal Psalm this week. But first, how does the reign of a king differ from the leadership of an elected president? What do kings have that presidents don't have? As Americans, it's hard for us to identify with royalty. We don't live under the authority of a king. What would it be like?

3. Now read Psalm 72 out loud. It's a bit confusing as to its authorship. The last verse of the psalm refers to David, but the author is listed as Solomon. Here's what Charles Spurgeon says on this in *The Treasury of David*:

   > Title. - A Psalm for Solomon. - The best linguists affirm that this should be rendered, of or by Solomon. There is not sufficient ground for the rendering for. It is pretty certain that the title declares Solomon to be the author of the Psalm, and yet from Psalm 72:20 it would seem that David uttered it in prayer before he died. With some diffidence we suggest that the spirit and matter of the Psalm are David's, but that he was too near his end to pen the words, or cast them into form; Solomon, therefore, caught his dying

father's song, fashioned it into goodly verse, and, without robbing his father, made the Psalm his own. It is, we conjecture, the Prayer of David, but the Psalm of Solomon. — biblehub.com

Do you agree with Spurgeon's commentary?

4. Find the themes in this psalm. What kind of king does David pray his son becomes? What character traits ought he to possess and nurture?

5. What could you extract from this psalm to use as a prayer for your own leaders?

6. Next, read Psalm 99 out loud. This is a psalm that exalts the King of kings. What attributes of God are listed in this psalm? How does God, the ultimate King, differ from earthly kings?

7. Read 1 Timothy 2:1-4. How should we pray for the leaders of our country? Do we have to agree with them in order to pray for them?

8. If there's time left, spend it in prayer for your church leaders and/or government officials on the local, state or national level. Use what you learned today as your guide.

Assignment for the coming week: Read Days 50-56, and write out your verse and response each day. Review all your responses before the next study, and choose which verse and response you'd like to share with the group.

Close in prayer.

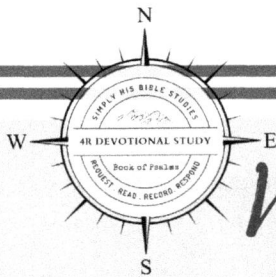

Come prepared to discuss the readings listed for Days 50-56.

Open in prayer.

1. Start by sharing with each other a favorite verse from your readings this past week. Talk about why it "mattered" to you and, if willing, share your response to the Lord about the verse.

2. Summarize the purpose for the Psalms of Ascent based on your reading last week. Share your favorite seasonal hymn or worship song from Christmas, Thanksgiving, or Easter. What moves you about that particular song or hymn?

3. One of the most famous of the Psalms of Ascent is Psalm 121. Read this psalm out loud.

4. The psalmist asks, "where does my help come from?" (vs. 1), then looks to the hills and realizes that creation itself is not the answer. Where do we tend to look for help instead of to the Lord?

5. The psalmist repeats the truth that God does not "slumber nor sleep" (vs. 4). Why do you think this particular reassurance was repeated?

6. What does it mean that "the LORD is your shade at your right hand" (vs. 5)?

7. How does God keep watch over us? How do we reconcile the promise that He keeps us from harm with the times when we surely feel harmed?

8. God watches over us. Think of a parent watching over a small child. What kind of focus must one give to a two-year-old? How are we in need of God's watch-care over us?

9. The Songs of Ascent were sung in unison. What is the value of singing songs together?

Assignment for the coming week: Read Days 57-63, and write out your verse and response each day. Review all your responses before the next study, and choose which verse and response you'd like to share with the group.

Next week will be the last meeting of our study. Take some time this week to reflect on what you have learned and come prepared to share at least two "take-aways" with the class—truths you particularly wish to remember.

Close in prayer.

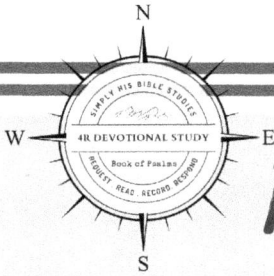

Week Nine Group Study

Come prepared to discuss the readings listed for Days 57-63.

Open in prayer.

1. Start by sharing with each other a favorite verse from your readings this past week. Talk about why it "mattered" to you and, if willing, share your response to the Lord about the verse.

2. We are going to examine an Imprecatory Psalm in this lesson. Read Psalm 140 out loud.

3. How does David describe the evil men? What does he want God to do to them?

4. Why do you think God wants us to read the imprecatory psalms, where David and others desire to see evil people punished?

5. Read Romans 12:18-19. What do we learn about God's administration of justice . . . and ours? What is the difference between wanting God to be just and wanting to take revenge ourselves? Have there been times when you have judged someone incorrectly? Can we simultaneously want justice while wanting our enemy to repent? How do we hold these two desires in tension with one another?

6. Do you have a favorite psalm or psalm-type after taking this course? What is it and why is it a favorite of yours?

7. What have you learned about prayer from the Psalms?

8. What have you learned about God from the Psalms?

9. What have you learned about daily time with God?

Close in prayer.

The following pages are provided as bonus space. Use the checklist if you are following the Read All the Psalms Plan. You can use the lined pages for lists if you are participating in the Additional Study Options or for extra space to write out what the Psalms are teaching you about God. If you run out of room—and you might—consider buying a little notebook and continuing your discoveries there!

Read All the Psalms Plan

☐ Psalm 1	☐ Psalm 31	☐ Psalm 61	☐ Psalm 91	☐ Psalm 121
☐ Psalm 2	☐ Psalm 32	☐ Psalm 62	☐ Psalm 92	☐ Psalm 122
☐ Psalm 3	☐ Psalm 33	☐ Psalm 63	☐ Psalm 93	☐ Psalm 123
☐ Psalm 4	☐ Psalm 34	☐ Psalm 64	☐ Psalm 94	☐ Psalm 124
☐ Psalm 5	☐ Psalm 35	☐ Psalm 65	☐ Psalm 95	☐ Psalm 125
☐ Psalm 6	☐ Psalm 36	☐ Psalm 66	☐ Psalm 96	☐ Psalm 126
☐ Psalm 7	☐ Psalm 37	☐ Psalm 67	☐ Psalm 97	☐ Psalm 127
☐ Psalm 8	☐ Psalm 38	☐ Psalm 68	☐ Psalm 98	☐ Psalm 128
☐ Psalm 9	☐ Psalm 39	☐ Psalm 69	☐ Psalm 99	☐ Psalm 129
☐ Psalm 10	☐ Psalm 40	☐ Psalm 70	☐ Psalm 100	☐ Psalm 130
☐ Psalm 11	☐ Psalm 41	☐ Psalm71	☐ Psalm 101	☐ Psalm 131
☐ Psalm 12	☐ Psalm 42	☐ Psalm72	☐ Psalm 102	☐ Psalm 132
☐ Psalm 13	☐ Psalm 43	☐ Psalm73	☐ Psalm 103	☐ Psalm 133
☐ Psalm 14	☐ Psalm 44	☐ Psalm74	☐ Psalm 104	☐ Psalm 134
☐ Psalm 15	☐ Psalm 45	☐ Psalm 75	☐ Psalm 105	☐ Psalm 135
☐ Psalm 16	☐ Psalm 46	☐ Psalm 76	☐ Psalm 106	☐ Psalm 136
☐ Psalm 17	☐ Psalm 47	☐ Psalm 77	☐ Psalm 107	☐ Psalm 137
☐ Psalm 18	☐ Psalm 48	☐ Psalm 78	☐ Psalm 108	☐ Psalm 138
☐ Psalm 19	☐ Psalm 49	☐ Psalm 79	☐ Psalm 109	☐ Psalm 139
☐ Psalm 20	☐ Psalm 50	☐ Psalm 80	☐ Psalm 110	☐ Psalm 140
☐ Psalm 21	☐ Psalm 51	☐ Psalm 81	☐ Psalm 111	☐ Psalm 141
☐ Psalm 22	☐ Psalm 52	☐ Psalm 82	☐ Psalm 112	☐ Psalm 142
☐ Psalm 23	☐ Psalm 53	☐ Psalm 83	☐ Psalm 113	☐ Psalm 143
☐ Psalm 24	☐ Psalm 54	☐ Psalm 84	☐ Psalm 114	☐ Psalm 144
☐ Psalm 25	☐ Psalm 55	☐ Psalm 85	☐ Psalm 115	☐ Psalm 145
☐ Psalm 26	☐ Psalm 56	☐ Psalm 86	☐ Psalm 116	☐ Psalm 146
☐ Psalm 27	☐ Psalm 57	☐ Psalm 87	☐ Psalm 117	☐ Psalm 147
☐ Psalm 28	☐ Psalm 58	☐ Psalm 88	☐ Psalm 118	☐ Psalm 148
☐ Psalm 29	☐ Psalm 59	☐ Psalm 89	☐ Psalm 119	☐ Psalm 149
☐ Psalm 30	☐ Psalm 60	☐ Psalm 90	☐ Psalm 120	☐ Psalm 150

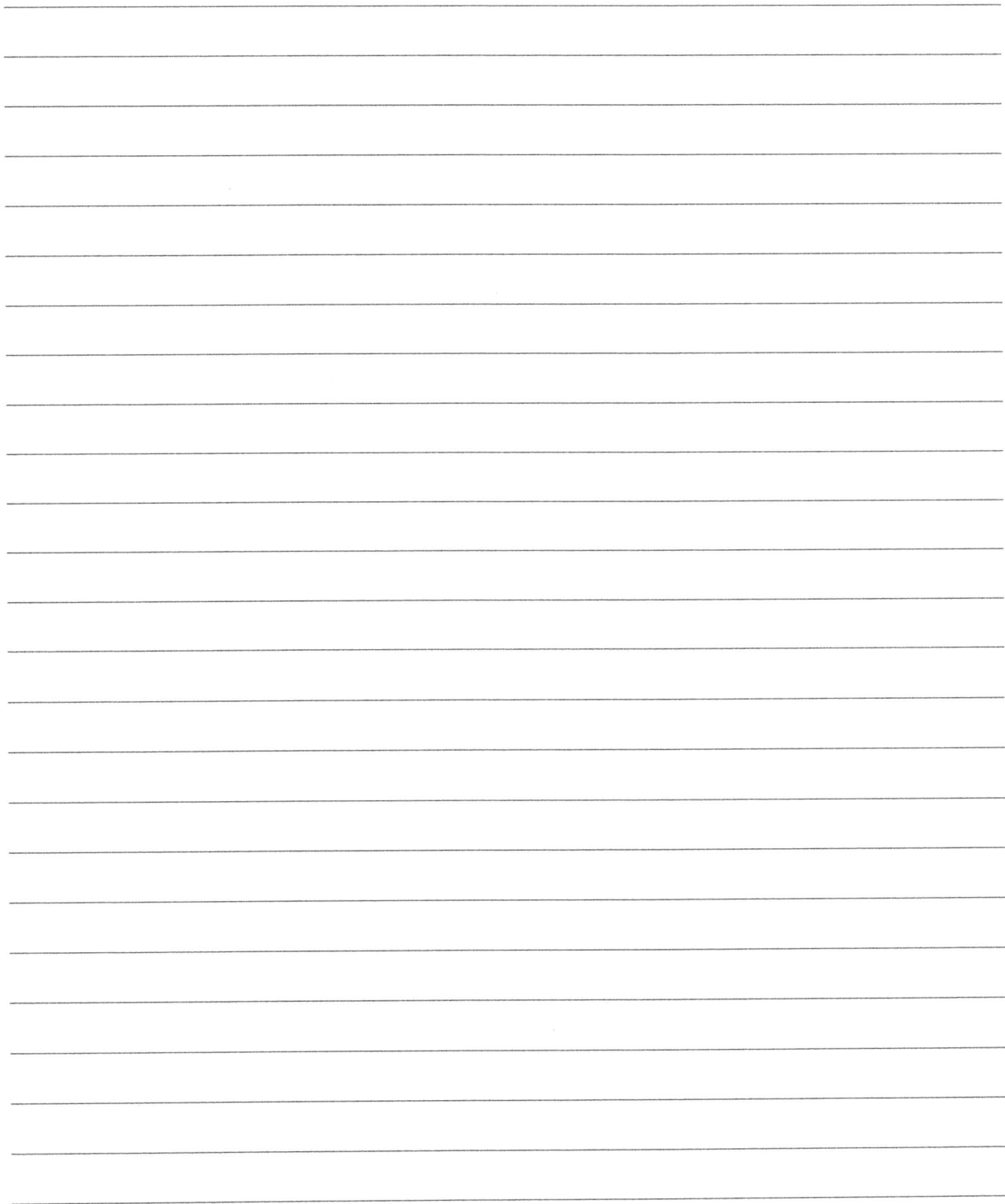

Meet the Author, Sharon Gamble

Hello, Dear Reader!

I wish we could get to know each other over a cup of tea, my favorite way to "meet" someone! Since that's unlikely, here's a bit about me and who I am.

I love people and excitement and parties. Especially tea parties with a few close friends. I also love quiet and creating space to be still with God. In fact, I've grown to love that most of all.

I think nearly all of us know very well without any help how to be busy. But fitting in intentional time to meet with God? That can be tricky. Sharing with women ways to find that time, to know Him more intimately, and grow to love Him more deeply is my passion and my happiness and my sweet spot for sure.

Throughout my life journey, I've collected quotes that have touched me and found Bible verses that have sustained me. I've learned truths that have shaped me. All that God is teaching me in the everyday stories of life, I'm thrilled to pass on to you with a grateful heart.

In fact, God stirred me to form Sweet Selah Ministries that I might share through writing and speaking the insight, thoughts, and lessons He is teaching me, especially focused on helping women stay close to the Lord through daily times in His Word and prayer. He has amazed me by bringing a team of women alongside me to help in this journey. Now, we have others also adding their gifts of writing and speaking to this growing ministry.

My husband and I live in beautiful New Hampshire with our little teddy bear pup, Bella Grace. We belong to a great church and love hanging out with our home group every other Friday night.

In the summer, we can often be found bicycling. We have a ton of winding, quaint back roads around here, and our bikes know them all. In the winter, we tromp in the snow and build fires in our fireplace and sip hot chocolate.

We are parents to two wonderful daughters and their dearly-loved husbands, and we are Nina and Papa to an ever-growing bunch of the sweetest grandkids ever.

Along the way, through the ups and downs have come life lessons:

> I've failed and learned that failure isn't fatal.
>
> I've overachieved myself into basket-case status.
>
> I've stumbled to God in a mess and felt His arms hold me close.
>
> I've seen the hand of God move in miraculous ways, over and over again.

I'm still on the journey of knowing Him better and loving Him more.

I'd love to stay connected with you. Write me anytime at sharon@sweetselah.org and sign up for our weekly email that will link you to our blog, "Monday Musings," our weekly "Tuesday Talks" on YouTube, our "Sweet Selah Moments Podcast," and so much more. You can also check it all out at our website, sweetselah.org, or join in on our app, sweetselahapp.org.

You are loved,
Sharon

Sharon has an amazing way of drawing her readers to the heart of God. It's as if she takes us by the hand and says, "Let's move in closer and see what it really feels like to be held by our Heavenly Father." She leads the way and lets us experience firsthand the depth of His love, His nearness, His power, His kindness, His sufficiency, and His care for us. He becomes so real as we spend time together and connect on a deeper level. If you want to get to know God in a more intimate, personal way, this is the book for you. I love all of her Bible studies and highly recommend them!

Nancy Lindgren, Founder and CEO
MORE Mentoring

Sharon's Bible study of the Psalms is a wonderful tool for anyone looking to begin or continue the wonderful habit of spending time with God on a daily basis. Sharon has a real gift of summarizing each Psalm for better understanding and giving helpful application that will impact the rest of your day. If you're looking for a devotional on the Psalms that is personal and powerful, you've found the right one!

Joel Beers, Pastor of Adults
Eliot Baptist Church

Held is like reading the Psalms with a wonderful, Jesus-loving friend beside you! This lovely Bible study is the perfect companion to walk you through this inspiring book of poetry and help you glean fresh truths from familiar words. A sparkling jewel of a book.

Lori Stanley Roeleveld, author of *Graceful Influence:*
Making a Lasting Impact through Lessons from Women of the Bible

In her personal, engaging way, Sharon Gamble invites the reader to join her on a journey through the Psalms, reading, reflecting and responding day-by-day. *Held* is a devotional guide not only for an individual reader, but is ready-to-go for a group study as well. Enjoy!

Larry E. McCall, author of *Grandparenting with Grace*
and *A Seasoned Marriage*

Sharon Gamble, the founder of Sweet Selah Ministries, never ever disappoints us! In her newest book, *Held*, Sharon invites readers of all ages to join her for a nine-week study (seven days per week) into the Book of Psalms. *Held* is more than a book, and it's much more than your average devotional. As you flip the pages and walk alongside the psalmists, you will sing and lament, worship and despair, all the while gaining an understanding of what it means to be held by the living God. And as with all of Sharon's books and devotions, there is humor, honesty, compassion, and grace. Always grace.

Sherry Schumann, President
Christian Grandparenting Network

Held.

A Bible Study of the Book of Psalms

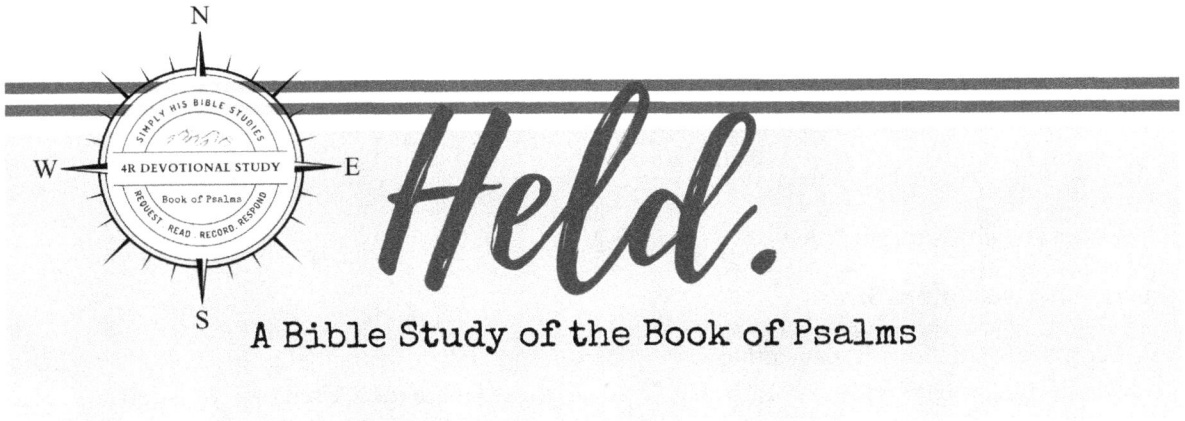

SHARON GAMBLE

Harris
House
Publishing

Held. A Bible Study of the Book of Psalms
Copyright 2024 by Sharon Gamble

Published by Harris House Publishing
harrishousepublishing.com
Arlington, Texas
USA

Edited by Judy Wilson and Marcia Aupperlee

Cover designed by Kathryn Bailey

Interior designed by Ben Santiago

ISBN: 978-1-946369-65-9

Subject Heading: BIBLE STUDIES / CHRISTIAN LIFE

Printed in the United States of America